POLITICAL EQUALITY IN A DEMOCRATIC SOCIETY

**Recent Titles in
Contributions in Women's Studies**

Female Soldiers—Combatants or Noncombatants? Historical and Contemporary Perspectives
Nancy Loring Goldman, editor

A Woman's Issue: The Politics of Family Law Reform in England
Dorothy M. Stetson

"Traitors to the Masculine Cause": The Men's Campaign for Women's Rights
Sylvia Strauss

Women in the Resistance and in the Holocaust: The Voices of Eyewitnesses
Vera Laska, editor

Saints and Shrews: Women and Aging in American Popular Film
Karen M. Stoddard

Women of the English Renaissance and Reformation
Retha M. Warnicke

Face to Face: Fathers, Mothers, Masters, Monsters—Essays for a Nonsexist Future
Meg McGavran Murray, editor

God's Handiwork: Images of Women in Early Germanic Literature
Richard J. Schrader

As Minority Becomes Majority: Federal Reaction to the Phenomenon of Women in the Work Force, 1920-1963
Judith Sealander

Women in Colonial Spanish American Literature: Literary Images
Julie Greer Johnson

Divorce and Remarriage: Problems, Adaptations, and Adjustments
Stan L. Albrecht, Howard M. Bahr, and Kristen L. Goodman

Women and Death: Linkages in Western Thought and Literature
Beth Ann Bassein

POLITICAL EQUALITY IN A DEMOCRATIC SOCIETY

Women in the United States

MARY LOU KENDRIGAN

Contributions in Women's Studies, Number 45

GREENWOOD PRESS
Westport, Connecticut • London, England

Library of Congress Cataloging in Publication Data

Kendrigan, Mary Lou.
   Political equality in a democratic society.

   (Contributions in women's studies, ISSN 0147-104X ; no. 45)
   Bibliography: p.
   Includes index.
   1. Women in politics—United States. 2. Feminists—United States—Attitudes. 3. Democracy. 4. Equality.
   I. Title. II. Series.
   HQ1236.K47   1984   305.4'2   83-12569
   ISBN 0-313-23775-1 (lib. bdg.)

Copyright © 1984 by Mary Lou Kendrigan

All rights reserved. No portion of this book may be reproduced, by any process or technique, without the express written consent of the publisher.

Library of Congress Catalog Card Number: 83-12569
ISBN: 0-313-23775-1
ISSN: 0147-104X

First published in 1984

Greenwood Press
A division of Congressional Information Service, Inc.
88 Post Road West
Westport, Connecticut 06881

Printed in the United States of America

10 9 8 7 6 5 4 3 2 1

For
Mae, Mike, and Margie

Contents

	Acknowledgments	ix
1	Introduction	3
2	The Nature of Political Inequality	25
3	The Impact of Social Change	47
4	Equality as Equality of Results	65
5	The Requirements of Political Equality	91
	Bibliography	123
	Index	145

Acknowledgments

My family and friends have made so many contributions to this book that I hope they are able to see a few of their additions as they read. I want to thank the Woodrow Wilson Foundation. The grant that I received from them was instrumental in the ultimate publication of this manuscript.

This book was begun while I was at the University of Wisconsin-Madison. During that time, Murray Edelman and Virginia Sapiro were very helpful through many readings of the initial version of this manuscript. I could never adequately express my intellectual debt to Booth Fowler. Without him, this book would not exist.

I want to also thank my colleagues in the Social Science Department at Michigan State University, Vince Lombardi and Ron Puhek. Jill Henderson and Cindy Hinckely have been indispensable as research assistants. Marlise McCammon has been friend, research assistant, and, in fact, ghost writer.

My hope is that the quality of the love, emotional support, and intellectual stimulation that I have received is in some way reflected in the quality of the book.

POLITICAL EQUALITY IN A DEMOCRATIC SOCIETY

1

Introduction

Questions concerning the value of political involvement are similar to questions concerning involvement in religion, sex, love, or the occult: there are very powerful arguments both for involvement and for abstinence. The purpose of this study is to assess what feminists want from politics, when they direct their attention toward politics.

Surely there is no place in which women's absence in the conduct of human affairs is more dramatic than in the political arena. An underlying presumption of much of the feminist literature is that politics is important for increased equality between the sexes. Feminist demands for equality, of course, involve more than equality in the political sphere. Politics is neither the only source of discrimination against women nor the only source of potential power for achieving more equality.[1] Nonetheless, politics is a most significant source of current discrimination and a potential avenue for dealing with many forms of gender discrimination.

It should not be surprising that equality has been a key demand of women and minorities in recent times. Equality has often been a rallying cry for persons who consider themselves to be oppressed. Furthermore democracy and equality have always been on intimate terms. When democracy seems to be held in high esteem, equality likewise is most often considered to be of value. Even the concept of equality between the sexes is not a new idea. In the mid-nineteenth century, John Stuart Mill asked for equality between the sexes.[2] Although feminists oftentimes disagree on what equality between the sexes would mean and about the methods necessary to achieve their goal, they do agree that equality is imperative and that women are not now accorded equal rights with men.

What is perhaps at least somewhat surprising, however, has been that the concept of equality recently has been used by opponents of programs fought for by women and minorities. Inequality and reverse discrimination have been claimed by those who oppose programs offered by minorities and women to end their oppression.[3] This twist of fate does not have to be discouraging. It can provide the opportunity to require that those who advocate equality be more clear as to what they mean. The terms sexual equality, equality between the sexes, or equality of gender are used regularly in feminist literature. Quite often, however, equality is applied without any analysis of its meaning, or it is defined in one sentence and then applied, or the definition that is used is not appropriate for the analysis that follows.[4] The feminist demands for political equality must be articulated in ways that clearly define the nature of the equality that is demanded. We need a clearer understanding of the substantive goals required for democratic equality if we are to provide equality between the sexes, equality for members of minority groups, and equality for other groups that have been discriminated against. This belief is based on the assumption that the nature of the values, goals, or standards do affect the society that holds them.[5] Feminist literature consistently demonstrates the reasons why perpetuation of the status quo—even with some tinkering—will mean that women will continue to remain excluded from the democratic ideal of equality. It is essential that those who advocate equality between the sexes realize that such equality requires that persons be treated differently in order to be treated equally. Thus, the only form of equality that will protect women is equality of results—when the results that are to be achieved are full citizenship in the society.

Are There Women's Issues?

The theory that women may not be adequately represented in public life when there are so few women public officials is based on the assumption that women hold in common certain basic interests and viewpoints that men are either incapable of representing or unwilling to represent. Do women share certain distinct interests and viewpoints which necessitate, for the sake of democracy, that women represent themselves?

Research indicates that gender is not a very accurate predictor of political attitudes. There are many issues that divide women's opinions.[6] In addition, on many contemporary political issues the attitudes of men and women are very similar.[7] This should be no more surprising than the findings that on most issues the concerns of black Americans are similar to those of white Americans. Black and white voters are equally concerned with the quality of education, rising prices, and crime in the streets. Yet on issues directly concerned with race relations there are more than statistically significant differences on the basis of race. Indeed, on questions about racial injustice, the causes of the urban riots, what occurred during the riots, or the consequences of the riots, the division of attitudes on the basis of race is almost absolute.[8]

Thus it is not accurate to ask general questions about attitudes on all public issues in order to investigate the adequacy of representation for blacks in an all-white representative government. Can a similar argument be made about women? Are there certain issues that differentiate persons on the basis of gender to the extent that adequate representation requires a sufficient number of members of both sexes in the "institutional arrangements" set up for representation?

Feminists are able to point to some evidence that supports the contention that women's interests need to be represented by women—or at least that women's interests are not represented without the participation of women in the process. One argument for the shared common interests of women as a group is based on the contrasting roles that society has traditionally assigned to women and men and consequently the different responsibilities the two sexes usually have.[9] These divergent responsibilities lead to dissimilar viewpoints between the sexes on certain political issues and alter the priorities they give to the allocation of some scarce resources.[10] As discussed in Chapters 2 and 3, woman's role in the family has been very different from man's role. These traditional roles have led to significant differences in public life as well. For example, conscription exposed most men but not women to the military. Perhaps this fact is reflected in the large gap between men's and women's attitudes about the propriety of the use of military force or of the desirability of governmental policies that might lead the country to war. For example, women are more in favor of the nuclear freeze.[11] Women also tend to be less supportive of the use of violence than men and more likely than men to see the United States' entry in World War II, Korea, and Vietnam as mistakes.[12] Women show greater opposition than men to universal military training, capital punishment, and the harsh punitive treatment of drug addicts. They favor gun control and support conservation and consumer causes more often than their male counterparts.[13]

A second reason for the shared common interests that set women apart as a group is the inferior social and economic statuses that women, like blacks, have occupied in this society.[14] The political, social, and economic discrimination that women face will be analyzed in Chapters 2 and 3. Several studies have indicated that the primary cause of occupational segregation and low wages paid to women is discrimination. One study indicated that the discrimination factor accounts for 83 percent of the earnings gap![15]

Blacks have argued for a long time that it is not in the interests of white officials to change the conditions that lead to black inferiority since whites profit from their cheap labor and their performance of menial tasks.[16] Hence blacks must represent themselves in Congress and other decision-making bodies if things are to be changed. In teaching about the inequalities of an educational system that serves the middle-class students much better than the working class or the poor, I am continually assured by middle-class students that they favor these inequities, or otherwise the competition they face would be even stronger! Likewise, it can be argued that men's interests would not be served by altering women's status in society.[17] Such changes would cause the competition for positions in professional schools and higher-status jobs to become even more intense than it is already. Most men profit from the free or inexpensive care of their children and home. Few busy women have not yearned at times to have a "wife"![18] Men also profit from the low wages usually paid to women and the more menial tasks women do outside the home. Poor southern whites could always feel that no matter how deprived their existence was, it was still better than that of the slaves. Similarly, no matter how inferior their status, men know that their status could be lower: They could be women.[19]

Further, the question of whether women's position on various issues of female concern differs from that of men is not the only question, nor even the most important one, that must be raised in discussing the issue of representation and women. Perhaps women do not differ in their opinion on certain issues that they *should* differ on. False consciousness is not a problem exclusive to oppressed groups. Indeed there is more than adequate evidence that people support things that are detrimental to their best interests. Nonetheless, oppression implies that the victimized learn to identify with the needs of their oppressor. Thus the more significant question to raise when discussing the concept of representation is not whether women's political opinions do differ from men's, although there is evidence to so indicate, but whether they *should*.

Feminists, of course, advance definitive answers to that question. But do they speak their answers in one voice? The meaning of feminism could easily be the subject of many volumes. Much of the disagreement among feminists is on issues that I will not handle. Many disagreements center around questions that, while they have a public dimension, are fundamentally personal issues or issues related to the job market. Certainly there are disagreements among feminists on questions of political equality. Nonetheless, there is enough fundamental agreement on the basic issues for it to be reasonable to deal with feminism as one movement. I believe it is intellectually more honest and politically most important to stress the common element.

Juliet Mitchell argues that the women's movement should be seen as one whole rather than as several factions. She believes that at this point it is necessary to stress the complexity of the political attitudes and actions that have to match the complexity of the problem of discrimination on the basis of sex. She reasons that "where one has to deal with the problem of oppression in every sector, there is room initially for all forms of political groups or attitudes."[20] Thus, although there are differences that must be considered, these differences should not stand in the way of the basic agreements that do exist. Furthermore, it is these basic agreements concerning the role of sexual oppression in shaping contemporary public life that make it possible to consider the women's movement under the single term *feminism*.

To focus on the disagreements rather than on the similarities provides an effective way to neutralize the importance of feminist critique of existing political inequalities. An understanding of those inequalities is intrinsically important. In addition, I am convinced that the feminist critique can be very useful in the depths of the questions raised by political equality on the basis of gender and the implications those questions have for democratic theory. Thus, feminist theory will be used to mean the order I have imposed on several individual arguments. Such an approach is necessary in order to evaluate the impact of feminism on democratic theory.

Why Political Participation?

Feminists see women's self-interest as similar to each other's and as different from that of men. Feminist analysis of the role that men can or should play in the representation of women's interests should be divided into two different aspects: the cause of women's political inequality and the necessary solution to existing political inequalities.

The Cause of Women's Political Inequality

Shulamith Firestone is most adamant in her case for the need for women to represent women's interests. She argues that men and women were indeed created different and unequally privileged. Nature provided men with the opportunity to oppress women, and men readily took advantage of the opportunity.[21] Thus, she sees the necessary goal of the contemporary feminist movement to be not just the elimination of male privilege but the elimination of the sex distinction itself; genital differences between the sexes would no longer matter in culture.[22] However, in order for genital differences no longer to have import, men would no longer have some— or a great deal—of the privileges they now possess.

Although the class system based on sex may have originated in the fundamental biological condition, feminists dare not presume that once the biological oppression has been swept away women and children will be freed. On the contrary, Firestone fears that the new technology, especially fertility control, may be used against them to reinforce the entrenched system of exploitation. She quotes Engels in the context of economic revolution: "It is the law of division of labor that lies at the basis of the division into classes." She continues his argument: "This division itself grew out of a fundamental biological division. But this does not prevent the ruling class, once having the upper hand, from turning its social leadership into an intensified exploitation of the masses."[23]

Not all feminists argue that all men are the cause of existing political inequalities. Although feminists would include women in their analysis of the powerless, they would not limit their analysis of the powerless to women. It is only some men, certainly not all, that have power.[24] According to Jo Freeman, it is in women's interest to identify with all disadvantaged people—male or female.[25] Juliet Mitchell argues that any theory that rests on the notion of undifferentiated male domination from the earliest times to the present is an oversimplification. It is to some extent equivalent to a worker seeing the employer himself as the only enemy because he seems directly responsible for the individual exploitation. It simply gives a theoretical form to the way oppression is usually experienced. The role of men in the exploitation of women is a factor that should neither be ignored nor taken to represent the total situation. Mitchell takes issue with the socialists who would argue that it is not men who are the oppressors but capitalists. She also disagrees with the radical feminists who do not consider the system in their analysis but simply see all men as the oppressors. According to Mitchell, the two interrelate and feminists are correct in their analysis of the role that men play as part of the overall oppression.[26] Thus Mitchell would argue that all women do share some aspects of oppression, regardless of their social class. Likewise, regardless of their social class, all men are oppressors, at least of "their" women.

The Necessary Solution to Existing Political Inequalities

Although feminists disagree on the extent of male culpability in the existing political inequalities, they do agree on the necessity of women solving their own problems. The one argument is that participation is *instrumentally* important. That is, political participation is necessary as a means of gaining sufficient control over decision making on the governmental level to make the changes necessary for women to enjoy equality with men.[27] The programs that particularly concern women require taking resources from those now in power—some men—and redistributing them to those who are now powerless—including women. To raise the aggregate pay of the country's full-time working women high enough so that the median pay for women would equal that of men would add at least $150 billion a year to civilian payrolls.[28] These kinds of programs will inevitably cause conflict. There is little reason for men simply to give women equality; it is essential for women to organize into effective political movements to seize their own equality.[29]

Surely, if it is argued that for women to gain they must lessen, or limit, the power now exercised by men, the need for women to represent women becomes more evident. If working-class demands are seen as demands for increases in material resources, then enlightened persons in industrial relations can argue that it is within the interests of the middle or upper classes to grant these concessions. The profits pie simply can be enlarged by stepping up production. Caring and sensitive members of the middle class can represent workers' interests fairly. If, however, the issue is defined as the need to gain more power over the conditions of one's life—as worker and/or women—it is more difficult to enlarge the pie. Under most circumstances, increases in power for one group require decreases in power for another. If this is the demand, then it becomes more important for the group to be represented by persons from its own ranks.[30]

Although men might be unwilling to give up their privileges, most feminists believe that men and women will be happier in a world where inequality on the basis of sex is eliminated.[31] Nonetheless, feminists do argue that there are significant differences in self-interest that differentiate the genders. The question of women representing women, however, does not have to rest on that issue. It might well be argued on lesser points. For instance, women have a more accurate knowledge than men of the legitimate needs of women in society.[32] Or perhaps it is important that more women be involved in the representative process because issues concerning women will have greater relevancy and will be handled with a greater sensitivity by women.[33]

A second argument emphasizes that participation is a good in itself. Everyone should participate in the decisions that affect his or her life.[34] Even if men can and will represent women's interests adequately, feminists argue that they should not. It is important that women exercise their voice on issues that are important to them. Surely, they will disagree among themselves. But until they are involved in the political processes, women as a whole are excluded from making decisions that have important effects in their lives. Such exclusion creates serious limitations on human development. It is only with identifying individual and personal problems as political that they are capable of being resolved. Furthermore, enormous self-confidence and human dignity can be achieved by working collectively to resolve seemingly irresolvable issues.

Feminists provide an important insight into public life by demonstrating that inequalities are regularly perpetuated by keeping the source of those inequities "in the closet," that is, removed from public exposure and ultimately from public or any other kind of solutions.[35] The issue of whether everything is or should be politicized is a very complex one.[36] Liberals often assume that increased politicization will cause an assault on individual liberty. Yet for groups that have little or no power, the reverse is true. If the oppression is not brought into public life, the oppression continues.

Certainly the quality of the private life should be and has been discussed by feminists. The expansion of the public domain will not necessarily lead to a contraction of private spheres. The issues involved here do not lead to a zero-sum game. If the quality of human life is to prosper, it is important to avoid false choices. It is possible that a better public sphere not only allows but also encourages a better private sphere as well. For example, to allow women the political right to control their own reproductive decisions does not destroy motherhood. The right of women to choose pregnancy or its termination may well enhance motherhood. Similarly, day-care centers—when they are good day-care centers—can add to the quality of family life. Shelters for battered women do not invade the privacy of the home. On the other hand, shelters for battered women, day-care centers, or the right to abortion cannot guarantee happy marriages, well-brought-up children, or satisfactory intimate relationships. Happy marriages, well-brought-up children, and satisfactory intimate relationships all take effort that must inevitably be seen as private effort. Nonetheless, none of these goals is available to those who are facing an unwanted pregnancy, an abusive husband, or some alternative care for their children. If political equality is to be achieved, the understanding of public life and, most specifically, of political life must be expanded.

Juliet Mitchell explains that the first symptom of oppression is the repression of words: "The state of suffering is so total and so assumed that it is not known to be there." Women's problems are not private and personal and neither are their solutions. She sees the first task of the women's liberation movement, like most political movements, to start with a series of complaints that are transformed into a political challenge to the social institutions. This process of transforming the personal into the political is consciousness raising. She offers as an illustration the example of a small group of women, one of whom decides to describe all her feelings connected with an abortion that she has had. In turn, other women also speak. If they have not had an abortion, they tell of their fears, problems, and so on. In this way a personal incident that was condemned to the oblivion of privacy is examined as a manifestation of the conditions all women experience; the personal is seen to be a crucial aspect of the political.[37]

Jo Freeman also believes that a successful women's movement requires a profound resocialization of women's view of themselves and the world. It is necessary for women to change attitudes that have been molded from birth and have limited their opportunities. They must ascertain the extent to which women have been denigrated in this society and how they have developed prejudices against themselves and other women.[38] Likewise, Freeman concurs with Mitchell that this redefining of politics is not unique to the women's movement. Social movements are one of the primary means of socializing conflict, that is, taking private disputes and making them political ones.[39] Murray Edelman explains:

> To politicize an issue is to define it as appropriate for public decision making: to take it for granted that people do not have the right to act autonomously and privately and to engender that belief in others. Which issues are seen as appropriate for private and which for public decision making is dependent on social cueing. How workers are paid and treated on the job has been regarded as an employer's prerogative at some times and places and has been politicized at others. The problematic status holds for matters of faith and morals, for every form of human behavior—from education of children to the appropriate sexual behavior between married persons.[40]

Shulamith Firestone sees the women's movement as unique in its redefining of the political. According to her, the feminist movement is the first to combine effectively the "personal" with the "political." It is developing a new way of relating, a new political style. But she also speaks of this new political style as one that will reconcile the personal—always the feminine prerogative—with the public—the world outside. With this union she sees "the world restored to its emotions and literally to its sense."[41] She argues that "revolutionary feminism is the only radical program that immediately cracks through the emotional strata underlying 'serious' politics, thus reintegrating the personal with the rational—the female principle with the male."[42] Firestone understands the goals of feminism to involve such fundamental changes in society that they demand a much larger conception of the political.[43]

A reason that has been given to explain much of the non-participation by women in the political processes is that politics is defined in such a manner as to have from little to no meaning for them.[44] One study found that although masculine people expressed more interest in the generic term "politics," feminine people showed more interest in issues such as women as candidates and public officials, abortion, and the equal rights amendment.[45] Other studies of female political participation have concluded that the basis for the assertion of male political dominance and the unwillingness to take female participation seriously derives from the definition of politics as a masculine activity. The matters of importance that supposedly sway women—such as, human needs for food, clothing, and shelter; adherence to consistent moral principles; the pre-emption of national concerns with human concerns; a rejection of war as rational—are simply not considered political.[46]

Traditionally, women have been treated differently in the public sphere which has reinforced political and other forms of inequality. Feminists now ask that women be treated differently in another way in order to be treated equally. They ask for laws providing maternity leave rights in employment, social security benefits for homemakers, tax deductions for housekeeping, child-care expenses for working parents, child-care centers, retraining programs for displaced homemakers, rape counselling centers, and homes for battered women. They ask for specific laws prohibiting discrimination on the basis of sex in education, granting of credit, employment, and job training programs.[47] To help ensure that these policies are enacted and are enforced in such a manner that they contribute to the lessening of existing inequalities, feminists necessarily urge increased political participation for women.

A major advantage of treating people the same is provided by its simplicity. H. L. Mencken once remarked, however, that for every difficult problem there is a quick and easy answer: quick, easy—and wrong. There is, of course, real danger involved in arguing that women have to be treated differently in order to be treated equally. In the past, differential treatment of women has exacerbated the inequalities on the basis of sex.[48] Treating people differently can only result in more, rather than less, equality if the people so treated have some political power. The isolation from most jobs that are interesting, challenging, and/or financially rewarding as well as the unequal pay for unequal work, the poor working conditions, and lack of benefits that women are forced to endure are certainly testimony to the lack of power. Indeed, it is the recognition of the pervasiveness of the victimization of women in the economy that has led many women to become feminists.[49]

Thus feminists demand that the political issues be expanded to take economic and social concerns into consideration as well. To argue that the political must be redefined, however, is not an argument that everything should be political. The concern should be the good life of the members of the community. The issues most appropriate to meet those goals should be the norm used to determine what is best handled in the public and the private sphere. This kind of norm is not, of course, an automatic guarantee of anything. Human life is a constantly changing experience. At one time, with extended families and less transient lifestyles, the public did not have to be as concerned about battered wives. In my mother's generation, if a husband beat his wife, he would have to answer to her brothers. Today the wife either has no brothers or else her brothers live too far away to provide any sanction against such excesses.

Further, in determining what is appropriate for the public realm, the most vulnerable members of society should be given the most serious consideration. This is well illustrated by the issue of reproductive rights. It certainly did not take a Supreme Court decision to ensure that right to women with money. It is the less financially secure who need the expansion of the definition of public to include the issue of reproductive rights. Similarly, a most pressing issue for poor black women is the problem of forced sterilization. Doctors and hospitals will not try to force sterilization upon well-educated white women. It, therefore, becomes difficult to get such a problem on the public agenda. As abortion was fifteen years ago, today forced sterilization is a question that provides private hell rather than public debate for many women who are poor and black.

The fact that the understanding of what is public must continually be an evolving concept is not restricted to issues that are gender specific. Industrial societies are going through massive restructuring of the relationship of work to the society. The front-line casualties have been the steel- and autoworkers. But they are only the beginning. If the shrinking of jobs in the steel or auto industry—or in institutions of higher education—is not to lead simply to individual catastrophes, dislocated workers must learn to expand their understanding of the public to find solutions to this economic restructuring that are more of a solution than unemployment compensation.

Although feminists do argue that all women share oppression in common, they do not underestimate the difficulty in making sisterhood a reality. Indeed, as surely as it is essential for those who are oppressed to unite for common political action, equally as surely vast forces operate to prevent such organization. Divisions are intensified both by differences in ideology and structural opposition to unity. The dimensions of oppression that women share in common are obscured by divisions of race and class. Economic differences are further compounded by the fact that women are taught to compete with other women. Women compete for the "best" man, the "nicest" home, the most "successful" kids. As Juliet Mitchell puts it: "Women directed from childhood towards marriage, living in a man's world, relate primarily to men and mainly competitively with each other."[50] Under such conditions, it is difficult for women to come together to change their situation. "In working-class jobs," she explains, "women are segregated in women's work. In middle-class jobs, on the other hand, women are isolated in a man's world." There is a real challenge involved in getting women with such totally different experiences to see their common interests as women. Since the woman worker does not take her own work seriously, she likewise does not take her sister workers seriously. Due to this it is almost impossible for women to join in the collective efforts that are essential if they are to improve their work situation.[51]

Collective action among women workers is also made more difficult because two groups of women are excluded from the work force. The first category of missing women is the more affluent women. This group's absence from the work force cuts down on the potential leadership of the women's movement. The other excluded category is women with young children. Absence from the work force during their twenties makes it harder, for example, for professional women to gain promotions. In addition, this absence of women takes place during the years when they normally would acquire their political values. Absence from the work force during this critical period makes it harder for women to define themselves in their work role.[52] Such lack of definition makes it more difficult to unionize women. Further, women who are not organized into unions are prevented from meeting with other women. Thus the initial drawback of women's lack of socialization during childbearing years limits the possibility of developing the consciousness necessary to valuing collective action. Then this early inhibition to an understanding of group identity is further reinforced by the lack of available opportunity for socialization once women are back on the job.[53] Women thus see themselves only as individuals. And as individuals they are helpless to gain any economic or political power.

Feminist Demands for Equality and Democratic Theory

This book will analyze the requirements that are necessary in order for a society to guarantee political equality between the sexes. Surely political equality is not the only value of a democratic society. Equality must be balanced against other values such as justice and national security. Nonetheless, equality is an important ingredient of a democratic society. Thus, it is important that feminist demands for equality be articulated in ways that clearly define the nature of the equality that is demanded. If the goal is a society in which being female is no longer sufficient justification for unequal treatment, then surely we must first understand what would be required of a society which guaranteed, supported, and encouraged equality between the sexes. I will not argue why equality is necessary—or desirable. That is a task that has been tackled often.[54] Nor will I argue that the goal of women or the goal of a democratic society is for complete equality.[55] The difficulty of that task would be so enormous as to border on the absurd. Furthermore, arguments for complete equality necessarily bring up controversies that lend confusion needlessly to an analysis of what I consider to be a more relevant question: What public policies lead to more and which to less equality between members of the society? My concern is not with the issue of absolute equality but rather with what policies would constitute greater equality.[56] I will attempt a clarification of the requirements of more political equality rather than attempting a justification of equality. In addition to limiting the discussion to the issue of greater instead of complete equality, this analysis will be directed to the issue of more equality between the sexes. In a world of so much inequality, it is difficult to get a handle on any issue of equality.[57]

One approach to an analysis of political inequality is to consider a group that knows it is not equal and to analyze what it perceives as the nature of the inequality and the conditions necessary for the elimination of those inequalities. It is my hope that this approach will contribute not only to an understanding of equality between the sexes but to an understanding as well of the kinds of policies that are necessary in order to achieve more equal citizenship for all persons who are now suffering from unequal treatment.

If political theory is to avoid arid abstractions and speak to and enhance humanness,[58] it must include in the dialogues on equality the voices of those who have experienced inequalities. There are problems of course. It is more difficult for those who have been disadvantaged to achieve intellectual sophistication. The tyranny of intellectual sophistication can be as significant a barrier to greater equality as the control of economic resources. Neither are randomly distributed in the society; qualifications are not "objective." It is much easier to have a flawless argument if the writer has had all the advantages of the intellectual and social institutions of the society. Further, it is intellectually easier to continue an already intellectually respectable discussion than it is to tread new ground.

I am convinced that the purity of intellectual argument has often been bought and to some extent is always bought. "Bought" does not, of course, mean totally lacking in value—it simply means of limited value. Furthermore, an analysis of equality that does not evaluate arguments that go "against the grain" from this perspective is intellectually dishonest. It is simply too easy to find flaws in the analysis. In a world of so much pain, truth and wisdom born in pain will certainly not have the same polish and erudition as wisdom developed in the leather chair, by the fireplace, in the book-lined, wood-paneled study by persons who have supportive parents, loyal wives, adoring children, research assistants, editors, and typists.

There are certainly limitations in any of the feminist arguments. For those reasons and because any discussion of such complex arguments as the meaning of equality exposes itself endlessly to such criticism,[59] I will not ignore the weaknesses but I will not dwell on them either. While I find insightful criticism useful for intellectual development, I also believe that it is necessary to see strengths where they exist and to use those strengths to build. It is, of course, impossible to build on weak ground. In order to use this material, useful evaluation is essential. I will evaluate, therefore, the contributions that feminist thought and research can make to substantive democratic theory.

I am convinced that a discussion of democratic theory is particularly useful from the perspective of disadvantaged groups; feminists provide this vantage point. Further, I am convinced that philosophic analysis is much stronger when it is grounded in empirical observations. I find most unfortunate the virtual divorce between normative and empirical analysis which is so prevalent in most of the social sciences today. Normative conclusions can never be reached simply with empirical observations. However, normative values must be compared and tested with the best understanding of the real world that empirical observations can make. Likewise empirical observations only have value to the extent that they can contribute to normative analysis. The contributions are more valuable when they are explicit.

In any discussion of political inequalities on the basis of gender, issues concerning social-psychological inequalities and/or economic inequalities quickly emerge as well. While the nature of existing inequalities is certainly more profound than the mere inventory of numbers, one of the contributions of the discussion of inequality on the basis of sex can be seen in the manner in which empirical analysis can support and further theory. Empirical studies of political participation by women lead to analysis of factors that are not traditionally considered political. For example, the issue of whether the family should be taken into consideration in any analysis of the political can be debated endlessly. There are certainly theoretical arguments on both sides of that issue. However, any analysis of the actual participation of women in public life simply cannot ignore the role women play in the family. As we shall see, there is no way to discuss the possibility of more equality for women in public life without discussing the family and the manner in which the traditional familial role limits women's options in public life.

It is tempting to try to unravel the nature of the relationship. Does political inequality lead to economic inequality? Is psychological inequality the underpinning of it all? Or is it really economic inequalities that lead to political and psychological inequalities? Ultimately I decided that this is similar to the proverbial question of what comes first, the chicken or the egg. I do not consider it begging the question to argue that all forms of inequality interact and reinforce each other. These inequalities are unavoidably intertwined. Any analysis that tried to indicate which inequality has priority is futile. More important, such an analysis takes attention away from the significance of the manner in which inequalities are interrelated and reinforce one another.

Thus, political equality between the sexes can be achieved only when, in fact, gender is irrelevant in evaluating a person's possibilities to function successfully in public life. In order for that goal to be realized, changes must also occur in the allocation of economic resources and in the traditionally private spheres of human relations as well. Furthermore, any analysis of equality that avoids these questions may well be clever manipulation of logic and language, but it is indeed an analysis of something other than political equality.

That discussion will be developed in Chapter 2 with an analysis of the existing political inequalities. Chapter 3 will argue that if change does not include some ability on the part of women to determine the nature of that change, then change will not lead to more equality. Indeed quite the reverse may be true. As bad as the existing situation is, social change may well lead to greater inequities on the basis of sex. Chapter 4 will be devoted to an analysis of the reasons why feminists must understand equality as equality of results if their objectives are to be met. Finally, in Chapter 5, the requirements of political equality will be described and the importance of those requirements for democratic theory will be discussed.

Notes

1. Jo Freeman, *The Politics of Women's Liberation* (New York: David McKay Company, 1975), p. 14.
2. John Stuart Mill and Harriet Taylor, *Essays on Sex Equality*, ed. and intro. Alice S. Rossi (Chicago: University of Chicago Press, 1971).
3. For example, Marshall Cohen, Thomas Nagel, and Thomas Scanlon, eds., *Equality and Preferential Treatment* (Princeton, N.J.: Princeton University Press, 1977); or Lisa Newton, "Reverse Discrimination as Unjustified," in *Sex Equality*, ed. Jane English (Englewood Cliffs, N.J.: Prentice-Hall, 1977).
4. See, for example, Alison Jaggar, "On Sexual Equality," or Onora O'Neill, "How Do We Know When Opportunities Are Equal?" both in English, *Sex Equality*; or Alice Rossi, "Sex Equality: The Beginning of Ideology," in *Masculine/Feminine: Readings in Sexual Mythology and the Liberation of Women*, ed. Betty and Theodore Roszak (New York: Harper Colophon Books, 1969).

All three of these articles are most useful for an understanding of equality between the sexes. I believe, however, that all three approaches would be more appropriate for an analysis of equality of results.

5. Any political philosophy must consider statements of fact, causal connections, formal implications, and the values of ends that a policy is designed to achieve. These factors, however, are logically distinct and it is important for any well-formulated political philosophy to be conscious of these distinctions. In other words, statements of what "is" surely must affect statements concerning what "should be"—but they are not the same kind of statements. Indeed statements of what "should be," that is, statements concerning the goals, standards, and values of a society, are intellectually significant in themselves. The primary task of the political philosopher is to analyze and clarify these goals, values, and standards with which the worth of actions and institutions in a society might be judged. See Robert Booth Fowler and Jeffery R. Orenstein, *Contemporary Issues in Political Theory* (New York: John Wiley & Sons, 1977).

6. Virginia Sapiro, "News from the Front: Intersex and Intergenerational Conflict over the Status of Women," *Western Political Quarterly* 33 (June 1980).

7. M. Kent Jennings and Norman Thomas, "Men and Women in Party Elites: Social Roles and Political Resources," *Midwest Journal of Political Science* 12 (November 1968); Richard G. Niemi, Roman Hedges, and M. Kent Jennings, "The Similarity of Husbands' and Wives' Political Views," *American Politics Quarterly* 5 (April 1977): 145; Marjorie Randon Hershey, "The Politics

of Androgyny? Sex Roles and Attitudes toward Women in Politics,'' *American Politics Quarterly* 5 (July 1977): 261-287.

8. Robert Blauner, "Whitewash over Watts," *Transaction* 3 (March-April 1966); Nathan S. Caplan and Jeffery Paige, "A Study of Ghetto Rioters," *Scientific American* 219 (August 1968); Robert M. Fogelson, "From Resentment to Confrontation: The Police, the Negroes, and the Outbreak of the Nineteen-Sixties Riots," *Political Science Quarterly* 83 (June 1968); Robert M. Fogelson, "Violence as Protest," in *Urban Riots, Violence, and Social Change*, ed. Robert Connery (New York: Vintage Books, 1967); Robert Hill and Robert Fogelson, "Who Riots? A Study of Participation in the 1967 Riots," *Supplemental Studies for the National Advisory Commission on Civil Disorders* (July 1968), pp. 221-243; J. R. Feagin, "Social Sources of Support for Violence and Nonviolence in the Negro Ghetto," *Social Problems* 15 (Spring 1968); Kurt Lang and Gladys Engel Lang, "Racial Disturbances as Collective Protest," *American Behavioral Scientist* 11 (March-April 1968): 11-13; Barrington Moore, "Thoughts on Violence and Democracy," in Connery, *Urban Riots, Violence, and Social Change*, pp. 3-15; E. D. Quarantelli and Russell Dynes, "Looting in Civil Disorders: An Index of Social Change," *American Behavioral Scientist* 11 (March-April 1968): 7-10; H. K. Nieburg, "Violence, Law, and Social Process," in *Riots and Rebellion: Civil Violence in the Urban Community*, ed. Lewis H. Masotti and Don R. Bowen (Beverly Hills, California: Sage, 1968), pp. 379-389; H. Edward Ransford, "Isolation, Powerlessness, and Violence: A Study of Attitudes and Participation in the Watts Riot," *American Journal of Sociology* 73 (March 1968).

9. Virginia Sapiro, "When Are Interests Interesting?" *American Political Science Review* 75, no. 3 (September 1981): 703-705.

10. Marcia Manning Lee, "Why Few Women Hold Public Office: Democracy and Sexual Roles," *Political Science Quarterly* 91 (Summer 1976):314.

11. Gloria Steinem, "Post-ERA Politics: Losing a Battle but Winning the War?" *Ms.*, January 1983, p. 65.

12. Susan C. Bourque and Jean Grossholtz, "Politics, an Unnatural Practice: Political Science Looks at Female Participation," *Politics and Society* 4 (Winter 1974): 258.

13. Hershey, "The Politics of Androgyny?"

14. Lee, "Why Few Women Hold Public Office," p. 314.

15. David L. Featherman and Robert M. Hauser, "Sexual Inequalities and Socioeconomic Achievement in the U.S., 1962-1973," *American Sociological Review* 41 (June 1976): 462-483; Marianne A. Ferber and Helen M. Lowry, "The Sex Difference in Earnings: A Reappraisal," *Industrial and Labor Relations Review* 29 (July 1976): 377-387; Francine D. Blau and Wallace E. Hendricks, "Occupational Segregation by Sex: Trends and Prospects," *Journal of Human Resources* 14 (Spring 1979): 197-210; Gary D. Brown, "Discrim-

ination and Pay Disparities between White Men and Women," *Monthly Labor Review* 101 (March 1978): 17-22.

16. Albert Szymanski, "Racism and Sexism as Functional Substitutes in the Labor Market," *Sociological Quarterly* 17 (Winter 1976): 65-73; also his "Racial Discrimination and White Gain," *American Sociological Review* 41 (June 1976): 403-414; Michael Reich, "Who Benefits from Racism? The Distribution among Whites of Gains and Losses from Racial Inequality," *Journal of Human Resources* 13 (Fall 1978):524-544.

17. Hershey, "Politics of Androgyny?," p. 284.

18. One feminist argues that life for men in the top strata of business and professional occupations has been possible only because those men have wives who are leading traditional lives as homemakers, doing double parent and household duties, and carrying the major burden of civic responsibilities. (Consider how difficult it would be for the top ranks of foreign service, college presidents, or public officials to function without the duties their wives perform.) See Rossi, "Sex Equality," p. 183.

19. Barbara Deckard and Howard Sherman, "Monopoly Power and Sex Discrimination," *Politics and Society* 4, no. 4 (1974): 480-481.

20. Juliet Mitchell, *Women's Estate* (New York: Vintage Books, 1970), p. 67.

21. Shulamith Firestone, *The Dialectic of Sex: The Case for Feminist Revolution* (New York: Bantam Books, 1970), p. 8.

22. Firestone, *Dialectic of Sex*, p. 11.

23. Firestone, *Dialectic of Sex*, p. 10.

24. Deckard and Sherman, "Monopoly Power and Sex Discrimination."

25. Freeman, *Politics*, p. 172.

26. Mitchell, *Women's Estate*, p. 130.

27. Freeman, *Politics*, p. 14.

28. Lee Smith, "The EEOC's Bold Foray into Job Evaluation," *Fortune* (September 11, 1978), p. 59.

29. Joyce Gelb and Marian Lief Palley, "Women and Interest Group Politics: A Case Study of the Equal Credit Opportunity Act," *American Politics Quarterly* 5 (July 1977); Firestone, *Dialectic of Sex*, p. 10.

30. Zillah Eisenstein, *The Radical Future of Liberal Feminism* (New York: Longman, 1981), p. 235.

31. Jean Bethke Elshtain, "Moral Woman/Immoral Man: The Public/Private Distinction and Its Political Ramifications," *Politics and Society* 4 (1974): 453-573.

32. Jo Freeman, ed., *Women: A Feminist Perspective* (Palo Alto, Calif.: Mayfield, 1975), p. 258. This point is also made by Sheila Rowbotham in *Women, Resistance, and Revolution* (New York: Vintage Books, 1974), pp. 168-169.

33. Hershey, "Politics of Androgyny?" pp. 261-287.
34. Freeman, *Politics*, p. 108.
35. Ellen Willis, "Betty Friedan's 'Second Stage': A Step Backward," *Nation* 223 (November 14, 1981), pp. 494-496; Firestone, *Dialectic of Sex*.
36. Elshtain, "Moral Woman/Immoral Man," pp. 453-573.
37. Mitchell, *Women's Estate*, pp. 59-63.
38. Freeman, *Politics*, p. 118.
39. Freeman, *Politics*, p. 5.
40. Murray Edelman, "The Language of Participation and the Language of Resistance," *Human Communication* 3, no. 2 (Winter 1977): 159.
41. Firestone, *Dialectic of Sex*, p. 3.
42. Firestone, *Dialectic of Sex*, p. 210.
43. Firestone, *Dialectic of Sex*, p. 1.
44. Kirsten Amundsen, *A New Look at the Silenced Majority: Women and American Democracy* (Englewood Cliffs, N.J.: Prentice-Hall, 1977), p. 137.
45. Hershey, "The Politics of Androgyny?" Masculine people were persons of either sex who identified with male sex roles as measured by the Bem Sex Role Inventory. Feminine people were persons of either sex who identified with female sex roles. These roles were determined by a list of forty characteristics, twenty of which were considered masculine and twenty feminine characteristics.
46. Bourque and Grossholtz, "Politics, an Unnatural Practice," p. 258.
47. Freeman, *Women*, p. 459.
48. Sheila Rothman, *Women's Proper Place* (New York: Basic Books, 1978).
49. Amundsen, *Silenced Majority*, p. 48.
50. Mitchell, *Women's Estate*, p. 59.
51. Mitchell, *Women's Estate*, p. 139
52. Mitchell, *Women's Estate*, p. 182.
53. Freeman, *Women*, p. 166.
54. Herbert Gans, *More Equality* (New York: Vintage Books, 1973); R. H. Tawney, *Equality* (New York: Harcourt, Brace & Company, 1929); Michael Walzer "In Defense of Equality," *Dissent*, 20 (Fall 1973); Michael Young, "Is Equality a Dream?" *Dissent* 20 (Fall 1973): 415-422.
55. "The major defect of complete equality is the defect of all single value conceptions: if equality is the all-encompassing goal, then all other goals, regardless of their desirability or necessity become lower in priority, and no society can function by pursuing one goal above all others. The full implementation of the principle of equality would, of course, often conflict with the full implementation of other principles. This fact is sometimes used as an argument against taking the concept of strong equality seriously. That argument would only be valid if it were irrational to adhere to a principle which cannot be fully implemented without its coming into conflict with other principles. There is nothing irrational in so doing; and if it were irrational so to do then

it would be very hard to hold to any principles at all.'' Brian Barry, *Political Argument* (New York: Humanities Press, 1965), p. 122.

56. Gans, *More Equality*, p. 67.
57. Mitchell, *Women's Estate*, p. 96.
58. Jean Bethke Elshtain, *Public Man, Private Woman* (Princeton, N.J.: Princeton University Press, 1981), pp. 348-353.
59. Jean Bethke Elshtain, ''The Feminist Movement and the Question of Equality,'' *Polity* 7 (Summer 1975): 453-454.

2

The Nature of Political Inequality

An adequate understanding of the requirements for political equality demands a proper analysis of existing inequalities. Feminists' claims concerning inequalities in the political sphere inevitably include discussions of the unequal allocation of economic resources and critiques of areas that have been traditionally defined in Western liberal thought as the private spheres of life as well. This chapter will be devoted to an analysis of political inequality between the sexes and the manner in which this political inequality is reinforced by social and economic factors.

Existing Political Inequalities

Although women are now a majority of the electorate, it was not until 1981 that a woman was nominated to the United States Supreme Court. There has never been a woman president and there have been very few women governors, senators, representatives, or state legislators. Women have been grossly underrepresented among the federal judgeships and in the higher levels of the federal bureaucracy, and few women have risen to prominence in the politics of local governments. Likewise, women are seldom found in decision-making positions in political party organizations.[1]

Further, although the statistics on women in public office give dramatic indications of the lack of political equality for women, the reality is even more unequal than the simple compilation of numbers would indicate. The offices women run for and hold are the less important offices.[2] Women have been found to have less influence and be less active than their male counterparts in whatever political bodies they serve. Women have been characterized as playing the role of "spectator"—a legislator without ambitions, political or otherwise.[3]

One reason for the limited effectiveness of the female officeholder is that women's tenure in office is usually very brief. Congresswomen so often gain office through appointment or elections after the deaths of their congressman husbands that the term "widow's mandate" has been coined to describe the phenomenon. Indeed, Nancy Landon Kassenbaum, elected to the United States Senate in 1978, was described by the press as the first woman ever to be elected to the Senate in her own right! One writer who did research on the "widow's mandate" found that widows were much more politically effective than myth would allow.[4] Nonetheless, even when women have been allowed some political success, it is often by such unfortunate circumstances as the death of their husbands. They are not then seen as effective, and in politics the perception of power is almost as important as the reality. In addition, few widows manage to win the ensuing elections. Yet it is not until the fourth term—and sometimes later—that a representative gains the recognition and influence among peers that she or he needs to be an effective legislator. Few women have gained enough seniority to be effective members of Congress.[5]

A second reason for women's political ineffectiveness is that when it comes to committee assignments and chairmanships, women representatives have over the years been disproportionately assigned to the lesser-status committees. An analysis of the Ninety-fourth Congress (first session, 1975) more than confirms this policy. No women were included in the House leadership as speaker, majority leader or whip, minority leader or whip, or caucus or conference chairs. In the prestigious and powerful committees of the House, the participation of women was even more minimal than the participation of women in the Congress as a whole. Only one woman was elevated to the chairmanship of a committee, but that committee was not endowed with great status or power.[6] There has been no significant change in the representation of women in leadership positions since that study.

Further, when it comes to the informal relationships so crucial to a successful political career, indications are strong that women are virtually excluded.[7] There is some controversy concerning both the amount of social segregation that women officeholders face and the significance of that isolation. This issue will be discussed further in Chapter 5. Nonetheless, the research on both Congressional and state legislators indicates that the accessibility of social interaction is limited for the few women who are elected to these offices.[8]

Mere presence in the corridors of power is not enough to ensure political effectiveness. While this is apparent in an analysis of women office holders, it becomes even more apparent in an investigation of women who are active in the political parties. Although women are conspicuously absent from public office, they are at the same time conspicuously present in political party activity. They are members of the "auxiliary." Political parties could not exist as we know them in this country without the work of the volunteer. It is in this role that women are very active in party politics. However, most women who hold any political office or position are likely to be in the local sphere or the intraparty offices. By far the most common role is that of the volunteer who pours coffee, rings door bells, licks envelopes, "mans" booths, and takes care of many of the other petty details that need to be done.[9]

Of course some women take on more prestigious jobs than pouring coffee. There are always women on any committee and as delegates to political conventions. They give speeches and are interviewed. Since their effectiveness in such positions is usually determined by men, it is not likely that these women will challenge "business as usual." Nor will they be openly feminist.[10] Indeed the odds are good that nine out of ten women will respond: "I am for women's rights but I am not a feminist."

Additionally, unlike male leaders, female party leaders use the political party as their only form of public activity. Women belong to and actively participate in significantly fewer community organizations other than their party activities than do their male counterparts. For most women who are politically active, participation in party politics resembles their participation in the family. That is, politics tends to be more a "labor of love, where the party, its candidates, and its program assume relatively greater importance than it does for men."[11] As within the traditional family, women are quite visible and very unequal.

It is not surprising that men expect to get something out of their party activity. Neither should it be surprising that women do not. Despite their efforts, the women politicians have not reaped the rewards and power potential that come with partisan public office, or even major party offices.[12] Even when a woman demonstrates a strong base of support, usually the party hierarchy is the last to see her potential as a candidate. The shortage of campaign funds also severely limits women's abilities to win public office; this is partially a result of not being taken seriously by politicians. Although party activists will go out to raise funds for the campaign of a rising young man, they are much less likely to do this for a woman.[13] Furthermore, when women are encouraged to run for office, it is often for offices they are unlikely to win.

In summary, no analysis of political inequality is complete with the mere inventory of the numbers that show the unequal comparisons. Political inequality goes much deeper than the fact that few women hold public office. In addition to the way in which women are excluded from politics, an analysis of inequality must include some understanding of how the system works to limit their effectiveness in lessening gender inequalities even when they are allowed to participate. Perhaps most significant and most challenging for democratic theory is the extent to which female citizens are unaware of the inequalities or accept the inevitable and/or claim they prefer conditions this way. According to Macpherson, most political theorists, including Rousseau, Burke, Mill and Marx have understood very well that the workability of any political system depends largely on how all the other institutions, social and economic, have shaped or might shape the people with whom and by whom the political system must operate. It has generally been seen that the most important way in which the whole bundle of social institutions and social relations shapes people as political actors is in the way they shape people's consciousness of themselves.[14]

One of the major contributions of feminists to contemporary democratic theory is that potential for revitalization of this understanding. It is important to realize that oppressed persons cannot function as equal citizens. The very nature of oppression makes it impossible. This acceptance of an inferior position is an important part of the costs of discrimination. It is a factor that democratic theory must take into consideration if it wishes to do more than justify the perpetuation of existing privileges. Thus an analysis of women's political inequality also requires an analysis of their social and economic inequalities.

The Social Dimension of Political Inequality

In a society that claims to value equality, the existence of grave inequalities and systematic subordination of major groups is rationalized on the basis of a common belief that members of this group are somehow "different." In Aristotle's Athens, slaves were thought to be different. In the Levellers' England, people without property were different. In the United States when the Declaration of Independence was drafted, both blacks and women were different.

While there are many similarities between women and others who have also been seen as inferior,[15] there are also some differences. Recently at least some women have been provided with an education that, although it has not been translated into economic equality, does provide better tools to articulate perceived injustices. Furthermore, women have been trained to express emotions. Thus women may be uniquely well situated to deal with the components of social inequality—a problem that is certainly not limited to inequality between the sexes.

Feminist theory deals extensively with the question of oppression. Oppression is difficult to identify by either the oppressor or the oppressed. Shulamith Firestone writes, "It makes [the oppressors] uncomfortable to know that the woman or the child or the black or the workman is grumbling; the oppressed groups must also appear to like their oppression—smiling and simpering though they may feel like hell inside. The smile of the child/woman is equivalent to the shuffle; it indicates acquiescence of the victim to his own oppression."[16] An integral aspect of all exploitation, therefore, is that the exploited love their exploitation. It is precisely the mark of extreme exploitation or degradation that those who suffer from it the most do not see themselves differently from how their exploiters see them. Either they do not reflect upon their situation at all or else they acquiesce passively in the role in which they have been cast. A great deal of the literature on women is concerned with those aspects of society that make both men and women unaware of existing inequalities.[17]

Oppressed persons cannot function as equal citizens. The very nature of oppression makes that impossible. This acceptance of an inferior position is an important part of the costs of discrimination. The most obvious illustration of the role of oppression in inhibiting political equality can be seen by an analysis of the use of the franchise to provide greater equality for women. In order that the vote be meaningful for any person, that person must be able to assess her or his position in society. Such an appraisal is, of course, quite difficult for most people. It is, however, impossible for those who have suffered systematic discrimination. If the vote is to be used to enlist government in the efforts to eliminate current discrimination on the basis of gender, women have to vote for those candidates and favor those programs that will accomplish these aims. When studies indicate that a majority of women favor no change in the current power status of women,[18] feminists necessarily direct us to investigate the manner in which the various institutions operate in society to make a majority of the citizens feel they deserve an inferior status. As one writer points out, "It is one thing to be forced to act against one's interests, it is quite another to think and believe against one's own interest."[19]

If the nature of existing political inequalities is to be fully understood, the factors that make women think and believe in ways that are against their own interests must be taken into consideration. In such an investigation, any analysis of the political must take issues into consideration that are traditionally assumed by liberals as removed from the public sphere. Failure to consider these factors will certainly condemn women to continued inequality. Furthermore, that inequality will have the support of many women.

Feminists argue that the factors that perpetuate political inequality for women can be divided into a discussion of the female nature and women's role in the family.

The Female Nature

The obvious biological differences between men and women have been extended to indicate other not-so-obvious temperamental differences that are presumed to be sex-related. "For women, although no longer for other groups in the society, biology is destiny," says Kirsten Amundsen. "The mere fact that she bears children and has menstrual periods makes her prey to hormonal influences that shape her temperament and abilities in certain distinct ways. Women are supposed to be more emotional than men, less able to apply logic to problems and situations, more conforming and less aggressive, but also more devious, and superior naturally in possession of that 'feminine' quality intuition."[20] Feminine qualities are used to legitimate the discrimination against women in politics and in the job market. On the basis of the knowledge that woman is less intellectually assertive, less ambitious, and more emotional than man, it becomes easier to treat women less seriously than men.[21] The myth of femininity is seen as the instrument for the oppression of women. Shulamith Firestone notes that "women, biologically distinguished from men, are culturally distinguished from being human."[22]

Since feminists believe that the cultural understanding of what is "feminine" contributes significantly to existing inequalities on the basis of gender, it becomes necessary to examine how this concept of femininity developed. The whole socialization process is geared to discouraging girls from involvement and success in pursuits that require ambition, daring, or inquisitiveness. Included in this socialization process are children's books, popular literature, the media, the educational process, the church, and peer groups.[23] Further, girls who, in opposition to parents, teachers, or peers, resist the traditional and limiting conception of the feminine also find it very difficult to find any female models either in history books, other educational texts, or real life.[24]

There is a great deal of ambivalence among feminists about the female nature and the male nature. Certainly there are some problems with the kind of socialization that boys receive. It would be quite frightening to think of a world in which both sexes learned to be competent, to hide their emotions, to make culture rather than to make love. Feminists, however, do acknowledge that "the conditions of women's oppression do condition women." No one can "inhabit a small and backward world without it doing something to them. Thus, though 'women are wonderful' and 'black is beautiful' are crucial elements in the struggle, they must go hand in hand with the knowledge of what oppression has done to retard women."[25]

Feminine traits have been held responsible for a considerable amount of the discrimination that women face in the job market and in politics.[26] Femininity requires that a woman be kind, cheerful, affectionate, sensitive, and nice. Masculinity requires a man to be tenacious, curious, ambitious, responsible, original, and competitive. Masculinity is closely connected with the qualities necessary for success. On the other hand, as Kirsten Amundsen explained, "the nonaggressive, highly emotional, submissive, cheerful, and affectionate member of the other sex—the 'natural' woman...—is perfectly suited to take second place."[27] Women are considered less intellectual, less serious, more emotional than men. It is expected that women will not be as aggressive nor as dedicated to their work. Women are expected to get lost in details and to lack the creative talents and drive expected of men.

Oppression leads to certain dysfunctional traits. Furthermore, it is considerably easier to keep women who have such traits in an inferior position. For example, women are deterred from pursuing traditionally male jobs because such jobs appear unfeminine.[28] Jobs that require being assertive, getting dirty, or simply working with men threaten a woman's female identity. It then becomes more understandable why women accept jobs that have been traditionally related to the work they do in the home. They serve others as flight attendants, waitresses, teachers, or nurses; they assist men as secretaries, dental assistants, research assistants. Women continue to do women's work; and of course, almost as part of the definition, women's work is lower in status and lower in pay.[29]

The results of such conditioning are also seen in politics. A large percentage of women still feel that seeking public office is an unfeminine pursuit. Many women express a negative sense of political competence. It is only very recently that women have begun to consider it proper for them to hold public office.[30] The feminine myth is not left behind even when women are able to overcome negative images and run for and be elected to public office. Women office holders spend more time serving their constituents and less time wheeling and dealing than do their male colleagues. Women office holders have less influence and are less active than their male peers in whatever political bodies they serve. Similarly, in political party activity, researchers find that women activists behave quite differently from men. Men use the parties to further their careers, women selflessly consider the political party to be an extension of their family role. They give and do not consider what they might get. It is not too surprising to learn they get very little, except the opportunity to serve.[31]

People who think little of themselves also think little of others who they believe resemble them. The research on women certainly supports this. Women think little of their own abilities and are suspicious of other women.[32] If women are to become more equal, it is essential that they work together. However, if women are to work together, they must overcome their prejudices against other women. Moreover, many of those prejudices are based on a considerable amount of empirical verification.

Women's Role in the Family

It is in their analysis of the role that the family plays in perpetuating inequalities that feminists most clearly illuminate the manner in which inequalities are interrelated and reinforce each other.

As with the issue of the feminine nature, the issue of the role the family does or should play in contemporary society is a very large topic.[33] The analysis here will be limited to feminist perceptions of the role the family has played in limiting women's ability to become equal citizens with men. Women have the cultural mandate to give priority to the family. Even when she is working, a woman is expected to be committed to her family first.[34] Because women are expected to have the major responsibilities of home and child care, much of the discrimination that women face in both jobs and in politics is assumed to be appropriate. Women are in occupations in which each individual worker is replaceable or defined as replaceable. They are not in occupations that are seen as demanding a full-time commitment, that require individual judgments and decision making.[35]

Employers will not hire women for the "life-time" jobs because of a belief that they are not attached to the labor market. Such expectations become self-fulfilling prophecies. By treating women who do become pregnant as if they have quit, thus forcing them to resign or to take mandatory leaves without disability coverage, sick leave, or retention of seniority, employers discourage women from having a commitment to their occupation.[36]

Much of the discrimination against pregnant women is less than subtle. Employers feel free to ask women if they are married or plan to be, if they intend to have children and what form of birth control they use. Women who have become pregnant have been fired or forced to take extended leaves of absence. They have been denied unemployment benefits when fired. Those on leave have lost seniority and had to start over as new employees at lower levels.[37] Furthermore, employers are unwilling to invest resources in on-the-job training for women. They resist placing women in training or management positions that will lead to higher pay.[38] Although the average married woman with children will spend about twenty-five years in the labor force, employers continue to view women as less stable workers than men.[39]

On the other hand, it is acceptable, even commendable, if middle-class women take jobs to help their husbands advance their careers by going to school, to help children go to college, or even to buy some extras for themselves or for Christmas presents.[40] Women are brought up to think of themselves primarily as mothers and wives. Even if a women is employed, it is still the husband's job that counts. The woman is just "helping out."[41] It is difficult to take a job seriously, if no one else does. Even when educations are comparable, families do not relocate for women to advance. Decisions to move are based on the husband's career opportunities.[42] Women's, but not men's, educational attainment has been limited by decisions to marry.[43] Due to the household responsibilities, women are often reluctant to apply for on-the-job training that employers are reluctant to provide. Women can thus anticipate twenty-five or more years of the least interesting, most tedious, lowest status, lowest paying dead-end jobs. Although lesser educational achievements and lack of on-the-job training are not adequate to explain the wage gap between men and women, they do reinforce the segregation of women into jobs considered feminine. Further, assignment to low-status jobs has reinforced the view of women within their own families as secondary earners. This subordinate status has meant that women are expected to do a disproportionate share of the housework and to perform unpaid services—like entertaining—to further their husband's careers. These demands, in turn, make it more difficult for women to compete on an equal basis with men in the most challenging and demanding jobs.[44]

The aspiration to public life thus would be unlikely among any persons who had been systematically cut off from challenging, demanding, high-status jobs. The lack of probability of recruitment to public office becomes even greater when those persons are also kept continually busy doing work that never ends, is never noticed, and is given no recognized economic value.

In addition, when women do decide to run for public office, family roles are still far more significant for them than they are for men. Women office holders are far more likely to assert the need for a supportive spouse.[45] While men remain in public life even when their wife and family prefer they not, women feel far more constrained to remain in public life only when their husband supports their political activities. However, marriage is not *the* crucial limitation on women's aspirations toward public office. Children are.

One study of attitudes toward candidates found that large numbers of voters perceive themselves as being open-minded toward women candidates until the issue of motherhood was brought into the analysis. A considerable number of such voters felt that women with small children would be less likely to receive their vote.[46] Another study of men and women participating in local politics concluded that the percentage of women holding public office is unlikely to increase by any substantial amount in the future unless radical changes occur in current sex-role assignments. This study concluded that the nature of sex roles (especially those related to child care) are such that they deny most women the ability to compete against men for elected public office in the United

States.[47] Child care responsibilities do not limit women from most political activities, except holding public office.[48] Another study of political party activity indicates that the inability of a person to gain public office severely limits her or his influence in other party activities as well.[49]

The importance of children as a factor in restricting women from running for public office is indicated by the low percentage of women running for office during child-bearing and child-rearing ages. There is a considerable increase in the number of women over fifty who run for public office. This is not the case for men.[50] Because of children, women often fail to gain the experience their male counterparts are acquiring. When they are free of the child-rearing responsibilities, they often lack the political sophistication necessary to compete against the more experienced men.[51]

The Economic Dimension

Although it is extensive, sexual inequality in political participation is perhaps not very dramatic. In the history of the human race, politics has been the luxury of the few. Most men today do not become politically active and certainly even fewer are politically effective. The costs of political and social inequality, however, become more apparent with an analysis of economic inequalities. Economic inequalities dramatically underline the distance between men and women and begin to clarify the price of being "born female."

As the issue of political participation requires an evaluation of the depths of current political inequality, so does an evaluation of economic inequalities require an evaluation of the pervasiveness of those inequities. By 1968, over half the women in the United States were in the work force, and 24.7 million women have joined the labor force just in the past two decades. Working does not, however, mean economic independence for most women. When women do work, they earn fifty-nine cents for every dollar made by men.[52] As there are very few women in high public office, there are also very few women who hold high-paying jobs. In 1982, only 2 percent of the working women earned twenty-five thousand dollars a year.[53] A woman college graduate can expect to earn less than a male elementary school graduate. The median income for female heads of households is less than half the median income for male-headed families. As John Rawls puts it, "It is indeed unconscionable that those who are at the same level of talent and ability and have the same willingness to use them are not provided the same prospect of reward, status, honor and the possibility for fulfilling work because of an accident of birth which ascribes a differential starting place to certain groups."[54]

At least part of the reason for the discrepancy between men's and women's wages is that women are often paid less than men for doing the same job. Although such discrimination is illegal, it is often disguised by giving men different job titles: women are cooks while men are chefs, women are hostesses while men are maitre d's, and women are secretaries while men are administrative assistants.[55]

Even when men and women share the same occupational category, distinctions of rank and function often maintain the income inequity. For example, men have the sales jobs that involve commissions. Women do not. Distinctions like this account in large part for the fact that in 1981 women sales workers earned on the average only 52 percent as much as male sales workers, while women college teachers earned 80 percent as much as their male colleagues, and women bank officers earned 60 percent as much as their male counterparts.[56]

There is considerable evidence to indicate that the frequency of overt economic discrimination that pays women less for doing the same work is substantial. Between 1968 and 1981, litigation under the Equal Pay Act resulted in the awarding of more than $33.5 million in back pay to nearly eighty-four thousand employees—most of whom were women.[57] Nonetheless, only approximately 18 percent of the differences in pay can be attributed to the lesser pay women received for doing the same job as men.[58]

This is because there are very few specific occupations that are truly integrated by sex. The major cause of economic inequality for women is the sex-segregated job market. A study of the census from 1900 to 1960 describes the nature of this segregation. The study shows that women have been concentrated in occupations not only where they are overrepresented but where they actually have been the majority. A low estimate for 1960 indicated at least 59 percent of women in the work force were in occupations where women constituted 70 percent or more of the workers.[59] More recent studies indicate no decline in the concentration of women in traditional fields. Half of all working women are in occupations that are over 70 percent female and more than one-quarter are in occupations that are over 95 percent female.[60]

As might be expected, the jobs traditionally designated as women's are not the most creative, most interesting, most challenging, most lucrative, nor of the highest status. Women work at the jobs that are usually the most tedious, where working conditions are bad and economic rewards are minimal. Wages paid to women performing women's jobs are low. Once a job is viewed as women's work, the job is undervalued and the wages paid to women performing those jobs are depressed.[61]

The pattern for professional women, while better than that of most women in unskilled jobs, is still oppressive. They either work in jobs dominated by women, in which case the entire profession is kept at a low status, or they are such a minute percentage of the profession that they are reduced to the "exceptional woman" role. It is hard for anyone who has not been in that position to understand the limitations: every accomplishment gets excessive and patronizing praise, every limitation gets even more excessive notice. Part of the strain is similar to that endured by anyone who is upwardly mobile.[62] If the upwardly mobile person happens to be a female in a profession not typically female, then, of course, the pressures are even more intense.

The economic oppression is cyclical: not only are the jobs into which women and minorities have been traditionally segregated lower-paying, but they are lower-paying jobs, in part at least, because they have been reserved for women and minorities.[63] Although jobs are clearly distinguished as men's or women's work, there is usually little intrinsic to the job itself that leads to the determination. A job that is clearly and exclusively women's work in one factory, town, or region may be just as clearly and exclusively men's work in another factory or region. But while some jobs have changed from men's work to women's work, the degree of occupational segregation has not changed appreciably since the turn of the century.[64]

Further, men and women who attain equally prestigious occupations do not attain equal occupational earning potential. Although the earnings of the males and females are both greater in male- than in female-dominated occupations, the earning potential of prestige-equivalent occupations differs because males tend to be clustered in occupations with greater income potential even within categories of prestige.[65]

Another characteristic of woman's work is similar to her role in the family: women are encouraged toward vicarious rather than direct achievements. The cheerleader, the secretary, the nurse, the dental assistant, the research assistant, and even the school teacher—whose success lies in the achievements of her students—exemplify indirect achievers.[66] The pattern of "instrumental" father and "expressive" mother is not substantially changed when the woman enters the job market.[67] Women are not to have social prestige on their own. The woman is to be the caretaker of the family whose prestige is determined by a man. They are to help men in their achievements.[68]

Women can be well qualified when they leave school, but their opportunities for higher education and further training, such as apprenticeships or full-time study, are less than half as good as men's.[69] Although, on the average, women obtain first jobs of considerably higher status than those of men, by mid-life men are in higher status occupations than women. The sorting of men and women into occupations suggests a complicated allocation process. Apparently both men and women rely heavily on their educational attainments for their first jobs. However, for later occupational placement, men depend increasingly on experience and decreasingly on educational achievement to obtain job advancements. Women, on the other hand, must continue to depend primarily on their educational qualifications for later occupational placement. Men clearly profit by their work experience in the labor market and tend to become upwardly mobile, while women tend to remain essentially at the same occupational level throughout their working careers.[70]

A partial explanation for this is that women are rarely put into positions of authority.[71] Women tend not to be in supervisory positions—especially positions where they would supervise male workers.[72] This is true in both blue-collar and white-collar positions.[73] The assignment of male supervisors to a predominantly female work force limits women's upward mobility. For most women's jobs there has been no financial ladder. The female curve of wages is almost flat, indicating that most women's jobs are dead-end, with little promotional opportunity and few instances in which wages increase as a function of time or seniority.[74]

Even the professions that women have primarily been allowed to enter provide little social mobility. Teachers and librarians offer the most striking illustrations of this principle. Women dominate these professions in numbers only. In status, salaries, and power the relatively few men in these occupations outrank their female colleagues persistently and dramatically. In elementary and secondary schools, for example, two-thirds of the teachers are women, but only one-third of the principals and other school administrators are women.[75] Among academic librarians there are nearly twice as many women as men. Yet not one of the large academic libraries in the United States is headed by a woman.[76] Similar male domination can be seen in social work.

Feminists criticize both the relative salaries of men and women and the actual salaries that women receive. What is more important even than the inequality or lack of justice involved in women's getting little over half the salary received by men is the fact that women do not get a living wage.[77] Women represent nearly two out of every three poor persons in the United States, and three out of every four persons receiving public assistance. The median salary for men is $20,260; for women $12,000—barely above the poverty line. Since the woman with a college education earns less on the average than a man with an eighth grade education, the opportunity for women with less than a college degree to earn a "living wage" is limited even more.

Conclusion

It is certainly not educational deficiencies that lead to women's economic plight. Women earn less than men at every level of educational attainment.[78] Forty-two percent of all women workers are in occupations that have higher than average median educational levels but lower than average median earnings.[79] Occupational segregation has had the largest effect on married, white, college graduates, and it accounts for nearly seventy percent of the wage differential.[80] Various economists have concluded that discrimination accounts for the earning gap: as much as 84 percent according to one estimate.[81] Discrimination keeps women from many occupations. It also places a lesser valuation on "women's work," whether done by women or men.[82] Further, such discrimination can be seen in all aspects of the job market.[83]

Clearly, women cannot combat such discrimination individually. The most obvious way to change the institutions would seem to be through political activity. Yet many of the same factors that inhibit progress for women in other institutions of the society operate similarly in the political sphere. Political effectiveness is easier for those who need less. Persons who have the income and education to be more effective politically also have the option to move to a different neighborhood if they do not like the local school. Persons who can afford a full-time housekeeper are not dependent on governmental support for day-care centers. Women of independent means do not seek shelter in homes for battered wives. Those who are limited in their political skills usually must also rely on the government for more.

Again, in the political institutions, all the parts interrelate to keep disadvantaged people disadvantaged. Contributions to political campaigns can help a person gain access to public officials. Women with fewer assets have fewer opportunities to effect public policy in that way.[84] It takes money to run a successful campaign for public office. Since women have less money, here again they are limited.[85] Money is also important for the effectiveness of pressure-group activities.

Another significant resource is time. Child-rearing responsibilities, when they are assumed to be the exclusive or primary responsibility of the mother, seriously inhibit women from having the flexibility of schedule that is essential to public officials.[86] Further, women are usually not employed at the kinds of jobs that allow time off for campaigns.[87]

Professional status also affects one's viability as a candidate, and affects a person's effectiveness once elected to a representative body. The professions that help candidates to get elected and help freshman legislators to get appointed to important committees are, of course, dominated by men.[88]

A further resource is a sense of competence. Studies of voting behavior indicate that women have a lesser sense of political competence, and that this feeling affects their willingness to run for public office.[89] Thus, women need access to public life in order to break the cycle of discrimination they now face. That cycle of discrimination makes it very difficult for women to enter public life as effective representatives of the interests of women.

Notes

1. As of January 1982, there were twenty-one women in the House of Representatives and two women Senators. There were no women governors. Thirteen percent of the state legislators were women. *Ms.* (January 1983), p. 66. Women constituted 5 percent of mayors in cities with populations over thirty thousand, 55 of the 682 Senate-confirmed presidential appointees, 48 of the 675 federal judges, and 2 of the 412 army generals. *Ms.* (December 1982): 78.

2. Wilma Rule, "Why Women Don't Run: The Critical Contextual Factors in Women's Legislative Recruitment," *Western Political Quarterly* 34 (March 1981): 60-77; Susan Welch and Albert K. Karnig, "Correlates of Female Office Holding in City Politics," *Journal of Politics* 41 (May 1979): 478-479.

3. For an excellent analysis and review of the literature on women's political participation, see Bonnie Cook Freeman, "Power, Patriarchy, and 'Political Primitives,' " in *Beyond Intellectual Sexism: A New Woman, New Reality*, ed. Joan I. Roberts (New York: David McKay Co., 1976), pp. 241-264. See particularly p. 253.

4. Diane D. Kincade, "Over His Dead Body: A Positive Perspective on Widows in the United States Congress," *Western Political Quarterly* 31 (1978): 96-104.

5. Kirsten Amundsen, *A New Look at the Silenced Majority: Women and American Democracy* (Englewood Cliffs, N.J.: Prentice-Hall, 1977), p. 64.

6. Amundsen, *Silenced Majority*, p. 66.

7. Amundsen, *Silenced Majority*, p. 67.

8. Irene Diamond, *Sex Roles in the State House* (New Haven, Conn.: Yale University Press, 1977); Jeane Kirkpatrick, "Representatives in the American National Conventions: The Case of 1972," *British Journal of Political Science* 5 (1975): 265-322.

9. Freeman, "Power, Patriarchy, and 'Political Primitives' "; Harold D. Clarke and Allan Kornberg, "Moving up the Political Escalator: Women Party Officials in the United States and Canada," *Journal of Politics* 41, no. 2 (May 1979): 442-477.

10. Freeman, "Power, Patriarchy, and 'Political Primitives,' " p. 253.

11. Edmund Constantini and Kenneth H. Craik, "Women as Politicians: The Social Background, Personality, and Political Careers of Female Party Leaders," *Journal of Social Issues* 28 (1972): 230.

12. Constantini and Craik, "Women as Politicians"; Susan Gluck Mezey, "Support for Women's Rights Policies: An Analysis of Local Politicians," *American Politics Quarterly* 6 (October 1978): 485-497; M. Kent Jennings and Barbara G. Farah, "Ideology, Gender and Political Action: A Cross-National Survey," *British Journal of Political Science* 10 (April 1980): 219-240.

13. Amundsen, *Silenced Majority*, p. 56.

14. C. B. Macpherson, *The Life and Times of Liberal Democracy* (London: Oxford University Press, 1977), pp. 4-5.

15. Amundsen, *Silenced Majority*, p. 98.

16. Shulamith Firestone, *The Dialectic of Sex: The Case for Feminist Revolution* (New York: Bantam Books, 1970), p. 96.

17. For example, see Vivian Gornick and Barbara K. Moran, eds., *Women in a Sexist Society* (New York: New American Library, 1971); Leslie B. Tanner, ed., *Voices from Women's Liberation* (New York: New American Library, 1970); Carolyn Heilbrun, *Toward a Recognition of Androgyny* (New York: Alfred A. Knopf, 1973); Mary Lou Thompson, ed., *Voices of the New Feminism* (Boston: Beacon Press, 1970); Betty and Theodore Roszak, eds., *Masculine/ Feminine: Readings in Sexual Mythology and the Liberation of Women* (New

York: Harper Colophon Books, 1969); also Jo Freeman, ed., *Women: A Feminist Perspective* (Palo Alto, Calif.: Mayfield, 1975).

18. Naomi Lynn, "Women in American Politics: An Overview," in Jo Freeman, *Women*, p. 382.

19. Virginia Sapiro, "Sex and Games: On Oppression and Rationality," *British Journal of Political Science* 9 (October 1979): 385-407.

20. Amundsen, *Silenced Majority*, p. 100.

21. Amundsen, *Silenced Majority*, p. 106.

22. Firestone, *Dialectic of Sex*, pp. 91, 205.

23. Amundsen, *Silenced Majority*, pp. 103, 107; Deborah Bachrach, "Women in Employment," *Clearinghouse Review/National Clearinghouse for Legal Services* 14 (February 1981): 1041-1047; Kathleen B. Boundy, "Sex Inequities in Education," *Clearinghouse Review/National Clearinghouse for Legal Services* 14 (February 1981): 1048-1056.

24. Amundsen, *Silenced Majority*, p. 110.

25. Juliet Mitchell, *Women's Estate* (New York: Vintage Books, 1970), p. 163.

26. Ralph Smith, *The Subtle Revolution* (Washington, D.C.: Urban Institute, 1979).

27. Amundsen, *Silenced Majority*, p. 102.

28. Mary H. Stevenson, "Women's Wages and Job Segregation," *Politics and Society* 4 (Fall 1973): 93.

29. Rose Lamb Coser and Gerald Rokoff, "Women in the Occupational World: Social Disruption and Conflict," *Social Problems* 18 (September 1971): 543.

30. Marcia Manning Lee, "Why Few Women Hold Public Office: Democracy and Sexual Roles," *Political Science Quarterly* 91 (Summer 1976): p. 307; Mezey, "Support for Women's Rights Policies," p. 495.

31. Constantini and Craik, "Women as Politicians," p. 230.

32. Amundsen, *Silenced Majority*, pp. 112-113.

33. Jean Bethke Elshtain, *The Family in Political Thought* (Amherst: University of Massachusetts Press, 1982); Vincent L. Lombardi, *Crisis in Marriage: Efforts toward Spiritual Transformation* (Washington, D.C.: University Press of America, 1981).

34. Coser and Rokoff, "Women in the Occupational World," p. 538.

35. Coser and Rokoff, "Women in the Occupational World," p. 551.

36. Ruth G. Blumrosen, "Wage Discrimination, Job Segregation, and Title VII of the Civil Rights Act of 1964," *University of Michigan Journal of Law Reform* 12 (Spring 1979): 451.

37. Patricia Huckle, "The Womb Factor: Pregnancy Policies and Employment of Women," *Western Political Quarterly*, 33 (June 1980): 116.

38. Mary Corcoran and Greg J. Duncan, "Work History, Labor Force At-

tachment, and Earnings Differences between the Races and Sexes," *Journal of Human Resources* 14 (Winter 1979): 4.

39. Smith, *Subtle Revolution*, pp. 58-59.

40. Coser and Rokoff, "Women in the Occupational World," p. 540.

41. Mitchell, *Women's Estate*, p. 139.

42. R. Paul Duncan and Carolyn Cummings Perrucci, "Dual Occupation Families and Migration," *American Sociological Review* 41 (April 1976): 252-261.

43. Margaret Mooney Marini, "The Transition to Adulthood: Sex Differences in Educational Attainment and Age at Marriage," *American Sociological Review* 43 (August 1978): 483-507.

44. Smith, *Subtle Revolution*, pp. 58-59; Mezey, "Support for Women's Rights Policies," p. 495.

45. Kirkpatrick, "Representatives"; Diamond, *Sex Roles*.

46. Ronald D. Hedlund, Patricia K. Freeman, Keith E. Hamm, and Robert M. Stein, "The Electability of Women Candidates: The Effects of Sex Role Stereotypes," *Journal of Politics* 41 (May 1979): 513-524.

47. Lee, "Why Few Women Hold Public Office," p. 297.

48. Lee, "Why Few Women Hold Public Office," p. 304.

49. Constantini and Craik, "Women as Politicians," p. 230.

50. Lee, "Why Few Women Hold Public Office," p. 304.

51. Lee, "Why Few Women Hold Public Office," p. 306.

52. *U.S. News and World Report*, "How Their Lives Are Changing," November 29, 1982, p. 55.

53. Susan Bolotin, "Voices from the Post Feminist Generation," *New York Times Magazine*, October 17, 1982, p. 107.

54. John Rawls, *A Theory of Justice* (Cambridge: Harvard University Press, Belknap Press, 1971), p. 73.

55. Blumrosen, "Wage Discrimination, Job Segregation, and Title VII," p. 407.

56. Barbara Ehrenreich and Karen Stallard, "The Nouveau Poor," *Ms.*, August 1982, p. 220.

57. Stevenson, "Women's Wages," p. 84.

58. Blumrosen, "Wage Discrimination, Job Segregation, and Title VII, p. 411; Bachrach, "Women in Employment," p. 1041.

59. Valerie Kincade Oppenheimer, "Demographic Influence on Female Employment and the Status of Women," in *Changing Woman in a Changing Society*, ed. Joan Huber (Chicago: University of Chicago Press, 1973), p. 198.

60. Bachrach, "Women in Employment," p. 1041.

61. Bachrach, "Women in Employment," p. 1045.

62. Judson Landis, *Sociology: Concepts and Characteristics* (Belmont, Calif.: Wadsworth Pub. Co., 1973), pp. 120-122.

63. Blumrosen, "Wage Discrimination, Job Segregation, and Title VII," p. 457.
64. Stevenson, "Women's Wages," pp. 86-87.
65. Steven D. McLaughlin, "Occupational Sex Identification and the Assessment of Male and Female Earnings Inequality," *American Sociological Review* 43 (December 1978): 920.
66. Smith, *Subtle Revolution*, p. 46.
67. Mitchell, *Women's Estate*, p. 145.
68. Coser and Rokoff, "Women in the Occupational World," pp. 540-541.
69. Mitchell, *Women's Estate*, p. 41.
70. William H. Sewell, "Social Mobility and Social Participation," *Annals of the American Academy of Political and Social Sciences* (January 1978): 234-235.
71. Smith, *Subtle Revolution*, p. 46.
72. Stevenson, "Women's Wages," p. 86.
73. Smith, *Subtle Revolution*, p. 48.
74. Blumrosen, "Wage Discrimination, Job Segregation, and Title VII," p. 412.
75. Smith, *Subtle Revolution*, p. 46.
76. Amundsen, *Silenced Majority*, p. 52.
77. Mitchell, *Women's Estate*, p. 138.
78. Bachrach, "Women in Employment," p. 1041.
79. Stevenson, "Women's Wages," p. 85.
80. Smith, *Subtle Revolution*, p. 49.
81. David L. Featherman and Robert M. Hauser, "Sexual Inequalities and Socioeconomic Achievement in the U.S., 1962-1973," *American Sociological Review* 41 (June 1976): 481.
82. Marianne A. Ferber and Helen M. Lowry, "The Sex Difference in Earnings: A Reappraisal," *Industrial and Labor Relations Review* 29 (July 1976): 381.
83. Gary D. Brown, "Discrimination and Pay Disparities between White Men and Women," *Monthly Labor Review* 101 (March 1978): 22.
84. Amundsen, *Silenced Majority*, p. 83.
85. Virginia Currey, "Campaign Theory and Practice: The Gender Variable," in *A Portrait of Marginality: Political Behavior of the American Woman*, ed. Marianne Githens and Jewel L. Prestage (New York: David McKay Company, 1977), p. 167.
86. Lee, "Why Few Women Hold Public Office."
87. Currey, "Campaign Theory and Practice," p. 161; Coser and Rokoff, "Women in the Occupational World," p. 543.
88. Marianne Githens, "Spectators, Agitators, or Lawmakers: Women in

State Legislatures,'' in Githens and Prestage, *Portrait of Marginality*, pp. 196-210.

89. Lee, ''Why Few Women Hold Public Office,'' p. 307; Rule, ''Why Women Don't Run,'' pp. 60-77.

3

The Impact of Social Change

A major theme running through the feminist literature is that, although inequality on the basis of sex is a constant in all societies at all times, recent social change provides an opportunity for abolition of this inequality. However, there is also another theme that at first may appear contradictory. Feminists also continually cite evidence and argue that, not only have the inequalities on the basis of sex not diminished, they have in fact increased! If this apparent contradiction is to be understood, any analysis of equality between the sexes must provide an understanding of the manner in which inequalities between the sexes is perpetuated and reinforced. It is precisely the advantage of the concepts of social stratification, institutional racism, and institutional sexism that they facilitate such an analysis.

Since past inequalities were so blatant, it is difficult to avoid the presumption that changes in the relationships between the sexes must, of course, include a movement toward more equality. Before developing the concept of institutional sexism, two illustrations of the impact of change on existing inequalities between the sexes will be provided. These include changes in the family and changes in the economy.

Changes in the Family

Feminists are often pictured as embittered women who wish to destroy the family unit. Certainly most feminists are serious critics of the contemporary family. The feminist critique that is best related to the impact of the family on political equality is twofold: 1) women's role in the family is a position of dependence, and 2) women's role in the family is seriously undervalued.

Feminists object to women's role in the family primarily because its position of dependence is both psychological and economic. Even if the woman is equally educated, even when she is working, she is rarely able to make a comparable salary to that of her husband, given the inequalities of the job market. In addition, when she bears and takes care of children, her dependency increases.[1] Though women may and often do share in the income and prestige accorded to their husbands, that income and prestige is his, not hers. If he leaves, the income and prestige leave with him.[2]

Women who do not work outside the home have no disability coverage, no unemployment compensation, and no retirement benefits independent of their spouses.[3] Divorced women can receive benefits only when their exhusbands reach sixty-two and decide to retire. Many older women who receive Social Security live in poverty. In fact, about 2.8 million women over the age of sixty-five live in poverty.[4]

Women's dependency in marriage, however, is not limited to economic dependency. Feminists believe that one obstacle to equality is the fact that women often consider themselves and other women less important than men. Much of the reason for this is attributed to the division that prevails in the family. The family social life centers around the career needs and the social interests of the husband. Families relocate when the husband's career requires it. The wife's needs are seldom taken into consideration in the important and often even the trivial decisions of the family. Such divisions are ego-destructive rather than ego-building.[5]

This kind of dependency sometimes leads to physical abuse—wife beating and/or marital rape.[6] It also leads to the problems of displaced housewives—women in their late forties, fifties, and older with no marketable skills, who find themselves, through divorce or death of their husbands, with no male to support them or to justify their existence.[7] Most important, such dependency always leads to stifled personal development, when such adult persons realistically assess their possibilities and come to the understanding that it will be very, very difficult for them to function as independent agents. Such realization makes it difficult to have a sense of self worth—or to respect others in similar situations.

Further, if women choose such independence, which is the presumed birthright of males, the social costs are enormous. The "normal" choices for women are emotional support from family and dependency, or independency and being alone. These are choices that men are not required to make. The nature of these choices also makes it very understandable why women do not wish to assess their situation realistically—and why they become very defensive about their social position.

Another objection to the role women play in the family is that it is seriously undervalued. The division between the roles of husband and wife is not simply a division of labor. It is a division based on inequality where one job is elevated to social importance and the other is reduced to social insignificance. According to Juliet Mitchell, women's role in the family can be and often is obfuscated by philosophical discussions of differences. "Women's role is not inferior to men's," so the argument goes. "It is merely different." Indeed, sometimes the argument is made that women's role in the family is superior! Mitchell compares this kind of argument to the "equal but separate" ideologies of southern racists.[8]

Women work very hard and the work they do is unnoticed and undervalued. Woman as housewife is an unsalaried worker, uncovered by any laws regulating either hours, benefits, or manner of work. The housework done by her is not recognized as sufficiently socially useful to require the governmental protection extended to other types of work.

Today, most women are employed outside the home. Since the housework and child-care responsibilities are still for the most part left to them, women are forced to manage two jobs. Employed women have been estimated to spend ten to fifteen hours a week on household labors,[9] most of which is tedious and invisible.[10] No recognition has been given of its economic value. Its contributions to the comfort of the household are seldom acknowledged until the services are removed. Women work hard and have no economic or other rewards to show for it.

In our credential-conscious world it is useful to consider the status in seeking jobs or credit that is afforded the woman who has been a successful housewife for twenty years. This person might well have been involved in dealing with much more money, managing more difficult personnel decisions, and involved in more complicated systems analysis than many junior executives. In the evaluating of credentials for jobs that require such talents, however, her experiences will most certainly be discounted. Indeed, she will be fortunate if she is able to get the utilities turned on in her name. Indeed, she would not have been able to without the necessary recent legislation. Further, decisions to ignore her contributions most certainly will be made by men who could speak eloquently in the abstract about the different but honorable position of the woman in the family.

At the same time, the work men do is considered of great significance—at least in their own home. The "man's home is his castle." There are simply no such castles built for most women. (Somehow if you have to build your own castle, it is not quite the same!) Today, women can no longer remain in "their" man's castle. They are forced to go out into the "real world." Their family role follows them there and limits their possibilities again for developing a sense of self-worth and/or independence. Women's role in the family ultimately determines their public role.

It may be appropriate for one parent to stay home and rear the children, but it should not *have* to be the mother. It also should be possible to have adequate child-care facilities so that neither parent would have to be involved in full-time child care.[11] In addition, women should be able to make an adequate salary so that marriage and maternity are not the only way out of poverty. Feminists demand that differences should not be based solely on gender; and even more important, they do not believe that the differences that perpetuate inequality should be allowed. This is the core of the feminist criticism of the traditional family.

It is certainly a cliché today to speak of changes in the family. The changes that are occurring, however, are not directed toward the problems in family life that feminists have cited. For example, the possibility for equality between the sexes, of course, is intimately connected with effective control of reproduction. Feminists presume the need to control pregnancy if equality between the sexes is to be achieved. The justification of gender roles leaned heavily on the subjection of women to the reproductive cycle. Although childbearing certainly is not totally voluntary today, it does become one option among others. Sexuality and pregnancy may now be separated for women as well as for men.

Feminists warn, however, that freeing women from the reproductive cycle will not by itself guarantee increased equality. If inequalities are lessened in one area, they may well be increased in another.[12] For example, as it became physically possible and socially desirable to have fewer children, the number of years that women have been freed from childbirth have come to be directed toward the "mothering" of the smaller number of children they do have. With the increased geographic mobility, the lessening role of the extended family, and the loss of siblings as sources of entertainment and as babysitters, the burden of mothering two children may actually be greater on the contemporary woman than the responsibilities formerly involved in rearing many more children.

It is not that feminists underestimate the importance of the socialization of children. On the contrary, they consider it too important to be used as a means of oppression for the mother. Juliet Mitchell argues that the attempt to force women's role exclusively on the rearing of children is harmful to the children as well as to the mother. The mother discharges her own frustrations, anxieties, and sense of helplessness on the child.[13] In the contemporary family, a full-time mother is only needed to the extent that the society does not provide the kind of support, such as child-care centers and flexible work schedules, that would allow women to be mothers and to have other adult options as well.

As economic pressures have intensified, the emphasis on socialization has diminished as increasing numbers of women with young children have entered or have never left the work force. By 1981, nearly one out of every two mothers of children under six were working outside the home. Nearly two-thirds of women with children between six and seventeen were working. This contrasts with ten years earlier when 30.3 percent of women with children under six and 49.2 percent of women with children from six to seventeen were in the work force.[14] Again, feminists argue that increased effectiveness of birth control methods has not made for equality between the sexes. Women may well have simply added part of the male's job to theirs. The time women formerly spent in having children, they now spend in "mothering" the children they have and in adding to the family income by working "on the side"— often forty hours a week in a difficult, boring, low-paying, dead-end job. All of this change occurred, of course, under the guise of "liberation."

Women today are not only working at low-paying jobs while they are rearing children, increasingly they are working at low-paying jobs and rearing children alone. Divorce rates in the United States have doubled in the past twenty years. Two out of every five marriages end in divorce. Fifty percent of all children can expect to live in one-parent homes for a significant part of their lives.[15] In addition to the increase of families headed by divorced women, there are also increasing numbers and proportions of never-married women who head families. A family consisting of a woman plus her dependent children is the fastest growing type of family in America.[16]

For mothers who become heads of households through divorce or abandonment, financial support from the fathers of their children is rare. In the United States, mothers are awarded custody in nine out of ten divorces that involve children. However, only 44 percent are awarded child support. Further, two-thirds of these women have so much trouble collecting the awarded payments that they eventually seek legal redress.[17]

Of the mothers working outside the home who head households with children less than 18 years old, more than one-quarter have incomes below the poverty line. The median income for female heads of households is less than half the median income for male-headed families.

Few feminists advocate the abolition of the family, but even those who do realize that there are worse alternatives for women. If a woman is forced out of her family status, with no other options, her economic and emotional situation can and does deteriorate even further. Clearly, change for women has involved increased possibilities for divorce and further opportunities for employment in low-paying, boring, and difficult jobs.

Changes in the Economy

Similar to changes in the family, changes in the economy will certainly lead to significant restructuring of women's roles. These changes will not necessarily lead to increased equality or more freedom. Change is written into the post-industrial society. If the nature of inequalities is not understood, however, that change simply will exploit further the persons who have been oppressed. Indeed, often that exploitation will appear as personal choice and be disguised as steps toward greater equality. Without political or economic power, women's function in the economy will be manipulated to meet needs other than those of the women involved.

In the past, women were encouraged to enter the work force when their labor was needed and were forced out of the labor market when the need no longer existed. Women were manipulated to meet the needs of the economy, and that trend seems to be continuing. After World War II, the available labor pool of single young women decreased. At the same time, the need increased for workers in occupations that had been considered "women's work." This led to a substantial overall increase in the women's salaries but also to major changes in the relationship between a woman's work experience and her family life. In other words, when women who were middle-aged and/or married were needed in the work force, it then became respectable for middle-aged and/or married women to work.[18]

As mentioned in Chapter 2, the number of women working in the United States has risen 95 percent or 24.7 million women, over the last two decades.[19] In 1982, 52.9 percent of the women were in the labor force as compared to 38 percent in 1962.[20] Among feminists this is seen as a hopeful trend. When women were considered as part of the family unit, they were also considered similar to children—as less than male, as inferior.[21] There is an underlying assumption that independence is better than dependence. Women need economic independence, and without an independent living wage, equality is impossible.[22] The hope is that increasing numbers of women in the labor force for increasing years might change the entire social system.[23]

If women are to achieve independence and not simply fatigue from their jobs, they must be paid an adequate salary. However, the difference between the salaries of men and women have changed little over time. As discussed earlier, the median income for full-time working women with college degrees is still lower than those of male high school dropouts. Women are still paid fifty-nine cents for every dollar paid to a male worker.

After almost twenty years of federal legislation prohibiting discrimination in compensation and segregation of jobs, the wage gap is as large now as it was before the legislation. This has been explained by the continuing predominance of women in lower-status jobs of a traditional nature, and the dynamic rise of women in the labor force which puts many new women workers at or near the entry level.[24]

Unfortunately, it is not simply that women are cut off from the jobs that are high-paying and provide opportunities for further promotions. Even more important than the inequality or lack of justice involved in women's getting little over half the salary received by men is the fact that women do not get a living wage.[25] In 1978, 21 percent of female-headed households with women in the work force had incomes below the poverty line.[26]

Working women in the United States comprise the largest and least known portion of the poor. A woman left alone to head her family is usually in a severe economic plight. Although she may work full time and in addition spend many hours a day keeping house and taking care of children, the median income for women who are heads of households is barely above the poverty threshold. This situation is all the more serious because it is a fate that may befall almost any woman at some point in her life. The aged poor, of which a clear majority are women, are the single most impoverished group in the subculture of poverty.[27] Since 1973, the distribution of women across the range of major occupations has shifted moderately. The Department of Labor reports six major job categories in which women have become the majority. Even in job categories where women are still a small minority, the percentage increases have been dramatic. There are more women insurance adjusters and women bill collectors. Also, there are dramatically more women physicians, lawyers, and judges.[28] However, the significance of most of the breakthroughs into the nontraditional jobs is often exaggerated. While women have increased their share of the higher-paying jobs at a rate slightly faster than their representation in total employment, most women are still going into traditionally segregated work.[29] In fact, despite the much-publicized increase of women in nontraditional jobs, the concentration of women in women's jobs seems to be increasing. The range and kinds of jobs open to women also continues to be restricted.[30]

Despite the large changes that have occurred in the extent of women's labor force participation, the degree of occupational segregation of the sexes has remained remarkably stable since the turn of the century. Occupational segregation is, however, rarely total. Between 1950 and 1960, highly segregated (predominantly female) occupations grew faster than less segregated occupations. Since then, there has been a decrease in occupational segregation as more men have moved into traditionally female professions and women have entered more typically male professions. However, while men moved primarily into the more prestigious female professions, such as elementary school teachers, librarians, nurses and social workers, the movement of women into male occupations was concentrated in sales and clerical jobs.[31] In addition, as more women entered clerical jobs, women's relative earnings dropped sharply as a proportion of men's earnings.[32]

Bank tellers offer a useful illustration of what can occur when large numbers of women enter previously male occupations. During the post-World War II period, one of the most startling complete "turnings" has been in the job of bank teller. Before the war, tellers were almost exclusively white men. The job had high prestige and was a step toward bank officer. Since that time, banks have been hiring women and minorities as tellers. Tellers' pay has not kept pace with other predominantly male jobs. In addition, the promotion ladder has been sawed off. Today future bank officers are more likely to be hired from recent college or MBA graduates than from among the tellers.[33]

Comparisons of various time periods, cultures, and even sections of the United States shows that the determination of work as women's work varies considerably. The factors that do not vary are the designation of certain jobs as work that should be done by women and the determination that women's work should be low in status and low in pay. Clearly the concentration of women in particular occupations is influenced by factors other than the inherent affinity of women for these particular types of work. In addition, the scarcity of women in other occupations is not due to their inability to perform the required tasks. Several scholars have concluded, after analysis of all the factors involved in determining wages, that discrimination is the major cause of lower earnings in women's occupations. Discrimination keeps women from many occupations. It also is involved in putting lower valuation on "women's work" whether done by women or men.[34]

If the increased entry of women into the work force is to create more equality between the sexes, women must have access to the higher-paying and higher-status positions. But how are they to gain such access? Incomes of males are more a function of their intelligence and ability than those of females. The incomes of black women are even less influenced by intelligence and ability than those of white women.[35] For both women and minority males, the return on an investment in education is considerably less per year of education than for majority males.[36] While increased education and occupational status do enable women to obtain higher incomes, these incomes are high only in regard to the incomes of other women and are not high in comparison with male incomes. The earnings gap widens for both majority women and minorities when the median number of school years completed is the same for men and women or minorities.[37] The process of earnings attainment is sharply different for the sexes, with men deriving greater benefits from their social origins, education, and occupational standings—even among persons of statistically equivalent work experience and levels of current labor force participation.[38]

Based on 1960 and 1970 census materials, the predictions indicate that the small decline in the relative importance of highly segregated male jobs between 1970 and 1985 will be offset by an increase in highly segregated female occupations.[39] As long as women continue to be channeled into traditionally structured segregated jobs identified as women's work, their entry-level pay will probably continue to approximate their average lifetime real earnings, with little prospect of longterm relative wage gains.[40]

Thus, while it appears that the expansion of job opportunities in the poorer paying and less desirable female occupations will be more than adequate in the near future, there is some doubt that expansion of the better female occupations will continue to provide equally good job opportunities for moderately or well-educated women as in the past.[41]

There are proportionately fewer and fewer jobs for more and more educated women. Women have been steadily driven out of the traditional "female" professions such as social work and primary and secondary teaching. Yet, because of the highly segregated nature of the job market, women have not been successful in integrating the "male" professions.[42] Since, at the same time, the options to marry and "live happily ever after" are diminishing in our society, it is difficult to predict what women will do.

Social Stratification, Institutional Racism, and Institutional Sexism

It is only with an understanding of social stratification, institutional racism, and institutional sexism that the pervasiveness of gender-based inequalities becomes clear enough to anticipate the results of social change. According to the Dictionary of the Social Sciences, "Social stratification is the differential ranking of the human individuals who compose a given social system and their treatment as superior and inferior relative to one another in certain socially important respects."[43]

A system of social stratification implies that social inequalities are connected: Inequalities in one dimension are related to inequalities in another. Further, the assumption is that these inequalities are interactive. The net effect of these inequalities is greater than the sum of individual inequalities. The normal functioning of the institutions in the society leads to the perpetuation of privilege. This perspective explains how the institutions of the society in their regular operations work to increase the inequalities already existing between the "haves" and the "have-nots." For example, people who can afford to live in the more affluent neighborhoods are able to provide their children with the best neighborhood schools with little financial sacrifice. Such children receive a better education, which is reinforced by cultural advantages in the home. These students qualify for the "right" institutions of higher education, where their parents can afford to send them. People who have had such training get entry-level positions of higher status, better salaries, and more opportunities for advancement. Likewise, those who cannot afford to live in the "right" kind of neighborhood, cannot "qualify" for the right schools, even if they could afford the costs. Thus, when scholarships are available, it becomes "difficult" to find qualified candidates eligible for the scholarship. Poor schooling leads to poor jobs with poor pay and little room for advancement. Thus, when after many well-publicized battles, well-paying jobs are opened to the formerly excluded, it is difficult to find well-qualified employees for the job. The inequalities are perpetuated and the system justifies and perpetuates itself. Jim Croce sang about the losing end of the stratification system in his "Car-Wash Blues." It is difficult to get an "executive position" if your experience has been at a car wash—or in rearing children. And it may be almost as difficult to think you deserve such a job as it is to gain the credentials.[44]

Most of the analysis of women in the social science literature has presumed that the class identity of a woman is the same as that of the male to whom she is attached, husband or father. Feminists argue that this is no longer an accurate assumption. Since most women are working for longer periods of time and since women who cannot or will not rely on a male for economic security and/or prestige find that in the job market the most relevant fact about them is their gender, it is important to study the role that sex identity plays in the stratification system.[45] One feminist writes that "it should be clear that a systematic hierarchy of social positions does exist in American society and we do treat the occupants of these positions as superior, equal or inferior in socially important respects." She argues that "sex is an enduring ascribed characteristic which a) has an effect upon the evaluation of persons and positions and b) is the basis for persisting sexual divisions of labor and sex-based inequalities." Similar to racial and ethnic distinctions, the sexual distinctions cut across all classes and ranks.[46] All women can thus be seen as comprising the same economic group. Furthermore, membership in this group—the criterion for which is only being a woman—puts all members at a considerable disadvantage in the political, economic, and social spheres.

By far the best indicator of the status a male will attain in American society is the status his father held.[47] It is not necessary to exaggerate the mobility for other groups in the society, however, to argue that the cycle that maintains privilege for the privileged and the lack of privilege for the underprivileged works with more rigidity for blacks and other minorities, and women, than white males. Stokely Carmichael and Charles Hamilton developed the concept of institutional racism to deal with the racial inequalities that continually derive from the ordinary operation of society's organizations and institutions and stem from the actions of established and respectable persons.[48] Kirsten Amundsen's concept of institutional sexism shows that the system functions similarly with women.[49] Institutional racism and institutional sexism are social stratification with a "double whammy." All of the society's institutions make it harder for the less privileged and make it most difficult or impossible for minorities and women.

As an illustration, social stratification would explain the manner in which all the institutions of the society obstructed Abraham Lincoln's possibilities of becoming president of the United States at the same time that they facilitated the possibilities of John Quincy Adams. Abraham Lincoln had not gone to the right prep schools or to Harvard. He did not have a father who could help him financially, give him advice, and use his influence in his son's behalf. Success was not impossible, but much more difficult, for Abraham Lincoln. It was only with a great deal of hard work and a considerable amount of luck that he achieved his success. Now consider the possibilities for Booker T. Washington and Susan B. Anthony! With all the hard work and luck they could muster, they could not have made it to the presidency—or even many positions of considerably lower status. They suffered the "double whammy." The evidence concerning the segregation of the job market on the basis of sex and the lack of social mobility available to women provides illustrations of the manner in which institutional sexism is a more rigid and more discriminatory form of social stratification. Occupational segregation stems from many sources: discrimination, cultural conditioning, and the personal desires of the women themselves. Women have been conditioned to believe that these often low-paying, low-status jobs are the only proper jobs for them. Furthermore, despite the statistics indicating that the majority of women work because of economic need, many employers still hold to the traditional view that men ought to be paid more than women.[50] In addition, because of their family responsibilities, many women prefer jobs that require little or no overtime work or traveling.[51]

Thus, it is not necessary that there be a deliberate or conscious conspiracy among male bosses and colleagues to prevent the advancement of women into more profitable fields—no more than admissions offices at major universities need to be composed of racists. The effectiveness of sexism on the labor market, as with racism, depends on the effectiveness of sexist differentiation and sexist controls in other institutions of the society. If, for instance, men and women are convinced that women are meant for a "different" role than men and are therefore not career-oriented, then it becomes much easier to fire a woman when the staff has to be cut back, to give the woman the dead-end job, or to relegate the woman to the job that pays less. Discriminatory behavior has become so well institutionalized that individuals generally do not have to exercise a choice consciously to operate in a racist or sexist manner.[52] The choices have already been prestructured. The individual has only to conform to the operating norms of the organization with which he is involved and the institution will do the discriminating for him.[53]

An analysis of both the existing inequalities and the direction of social change requires an analysis of the manner in which the interconnections between the various institutions in the society operate to perpetuate the existing discrimination against women. As with social stratification, institutional racism and institutional sexism are useful analytical devices because they direct the analyst to examine how the various institutions interact with each other and reinforce each other's influence. If, for instance, bankers, realtors, and the Federal Housing Authority believe that a racially homogeneous neighborhood is a more financially sound neighborhood, and if school financing is based on the local property tax, admission offices at universities do not have to be composed of followers of Lester Maddox or members of the Ku Klux Klan to enact racist policies. When the social institutions operate in the normal manner, privilege on the basis of race continues to be reinforced. The discrimination women suffer is similar to the discrimination involved in institutional racism. The social, political, and psychological pressures that tend to maintain the normal divisions of class operate at an even more intense level of suppression for women and blacks. Occupational and educational achievements relegate the victim of racism and/or sexism to a substratum within the major stratum to which he or she belongs.[54]

Conclusion

Social stratification, institutional racism, and institutional sexism reveal little about the absolute progress of the poor, of minorities, or of women, for this depends on factors external to such an analysis. If the economy improves or declines, the absolute condition of these groups improves or declines. These concepts are quite useful, however, in predicting the relative rankings of the various groups in the society. Social stratification, institutional racism, and institutional sexism clearly delineate the ways in which qualifications work to maintain the present system of discrimination into the future. Social change will allow some "super-women" and/or "tokens" to make it, as it has provided increasing opportunities for middle-class blacks since the late 1960s. The measures of socioeconomic change among blacks in that period show clearly the goals that the women's movement can hope to achieve at best unless the nature of existing inequalities is clearly understood.[55] Larger numbers of blacks are in the middle class than ever before, and those individuals have made significant and rapid progress. For the majority of blacks, however, poverty has become worse in both a relative and absolute sense. Furthermore, since the perceptions of most whites has been that the blacks are getting all the advantages from government, when dealing with a college classmate who is black and is having trouble in organic chemistry, the "average" white middle-class student—who has had at least three times as much money spent on his formal education up to this point, not to mention other "cultural" advantages—feels justified in his racist superiority. It is no wonder that it has recently become fashionable to be a racist again.

Thus, any analysis of equality between the sexes must begin with an understanding of what society is doing continually to increase the inequalities on the basis of sex. Such an understanding of the continued propensity of institutions to increase existing inequalities is not only essential for a reasonable analysis of inequalities between the sexes but is significant for an understanding of the operations of all inequalities in an organized, industrial society. If change continues to be confused with progress toward equality, some women who can prove themselves "as good as a man" will achieve at least some economic opportunities. Most women, however, will become more economically disadvantaged in comparison to men. The measures of women's economic situation vis-à-vis men since the 1960s substantiates this kind of trend. The degree of disadvantage will depend on the functioning of the economy.

If the economy continues to deteriorate, the economic situation of women will certainly deteriorate even more rapidly. And as with racism, soon it will again be acceptable to be a sexist. After all, women had their chance! The increase in sexism will probably not have the drama of the Miami riots; the peculiar sadness of gender discrimination is that it does not even get the notice of an urban riot. The agony of increased sexism will simply work itself out in the day-to-day misery in the lives of persons who have had the misfortune of being born the wrong sex. They will try to raise children alone as they battle daily to pay the bills, waiting for their dead-end, low-paying job to be eliminated.

Notes

1. Shulamith Firestone, *The Dialectic of Sex: The Case for Feminist Revolution* (New York: Bantam Books, 1970), p.48; Patricia Huckle, "The Womb Factor: Pregnancy Policies and Employment of Women," *Western Political Quarterly* 33 (June 1980).

2. Rose Lamb Coser and Gerald Rokoff, "Women in the Occupational World: Social Disruption and Conflict," *Social Problems* 18 (September 1971): 586; Kirsten Amundsen, *A New Look at the Silenced Majority: Women and American Democracy* (Englewood Cliffs, N.J.: Prentice-Hall, 1977), pp. 50-51; Roxanne Barton Conlin, "The Legal Status of Homemakers in Michigan," Homemakers Committee, National Commission on the Observance of International Women's Year, June 1977; Carolyn P. Edwards and Beatrice B. Whiting, "Women and Dependency," *Politics and Society* 4, no. 3 (1974).

3. Laurie Woods, "The Challenge Facing Legal Services in the Eighties," December 15, 1981 (unpublished).

4. Hilda Kahne, "Aid Old Poor Women," *New York Times*, February 1, 1983.

5. Marge Piercy, *Small Changes* (New York: Fawcett Crest Books, 1972).

6. Juliet Mitchell, *Women's Estate* (New York: Vintage Books, 1970), p. 100.

7. Conlin, "Homemakers."

8. Mitchell, *Women's Estate*, p. 105.

9. Kathleen Newland, "Women, Men, and the Division of Labor," *Worldwatch Paper* 37 (May 1980): 29.
10. Zillah Eisenstein, *The Radical Future of Liberal Feminism* (New York: Longman, 1981), p. 202; Amundsen, *Silenced Majority*, pp. 50-51; Mitchell, *Women's Estate*, p. 145.
11. Sheila Rothman, *Women's Proper Place* (New York: Basic Books, 1978).
12. Mitchell, *Women's Estate*, p. 118.
13. Mitchell, *Women's Estate*, p. 174.
14. *Newsweek*, "Death of the Family," January 17, 1983, p. 30.
15. Diana Pearce and Harriette McAdoo, *Women and Children: Alone and in Poverty* (Washington, D.C.: Catholic University Law School, 1982).
16. Beverly L. Johnson, "Women Who Head Families, 1970-77: Their Numbers Rose, Income Lagged," *Monthly Labor Review* 101 (February 1978): 32.
17. Newland, "Division of Labor," p. 29.
18. Valerie Kincade Oppenheimer, "Demographic Influence on Female Employment and the Status of Women," in *Changing Woman in a Changing Society*, ed. Joan Huber (Chicago: University of Chicago Press, 1973), p. 185.
19. Frank J. Prial, "Women Making Inroads on Traditional Jobs of Men," *New York Times*, November 15, 1983.
20. *U.S. News and World Report*, "How Their Lives Are Changing," November 29, 1982, p. 55.
21. Amundsen, *Silenced Majority*, p. 51; Mitchell, *Women's Estate*, p. 182; Firestone, *Dialectic of Sex*, p. 97; Jo Freeman, *The Politics of Women's Liberation* (New York: David McKay Company, 1975), p. 34.
22. Mitchell, *Women's Estate*, p. 182; Firestone, *Dialectic of Sex*, p. 97; Freeman, *Politics*, p. 34; See also, Karen Oppenheim Mason, John L. Czajka, and Sara Arbor, "Change in U.S. Women's Sex-Role Attitudes, 1964-1974," *American Sociological Review* 41 (August 1976): 573-596.
23. Amundsen, *Silenced Majority*, p. 51.
24. Ruth G. Blumrosen, "Wage Discrimination, Job Segregation, and Title VII of the Civil Rights Act of 1964," *University of Michigan Journal of Law Reform* 12 (Spring 1979): 411.
25. Mitchell, *Women's Estate*, p. 138.
26. Pearce and McAdoo, *Women and Children*, p. 5.
27. Amundsen, *Silenced Majority*, pp. 27-29.
28. Prial, "Women Making Inroads."
29. Blumrosen, "Wage Discrimination, Job Segregation, and Title VII," p. 413.
30. Blumrosen, "Wage Discrimination, Job Segregation, and Title VII," pp. 405-406.
31. Francine D. Blau and Wallace E. Hendricks, "Occupational Segregation

by Sex: Trends and Prospects," *Journal of Human Resources* 14 (Spring 1979): 206.

32. In 1973, the median wage for women clerical workers was 61 percent of that for men employed in clerical work; the proportion was 69 percent in 1962 and 72 percent in 1956. Blumrosen, "Wage Discrimination, Job Segregation, and Title VII," p. 412.

33. Blumrosen, "Wage Discrimination, Job Segregation, and Title VII," p. 408.

34. Marianne A. Ferber and Helen M. Lowry, "The Sex Difference in Earnings: A Reappraisal," *Industrial and Labor Relations Review* 29 (July 1976): 381.

35. Mary Elizabeth Ayella and John B. Williamson, "The Social Mobility of Women: A Causal Model of Socioeconomic Success," *Sociological Quarterly* 17 (Autumn 1976): 550-551.

36. Blumrosen, "Wage Discrimination, Job Segregation, and Title VII," p. 414.

37. Blumrosen, "Wage Discrimination, Job Segregation, and Title VII," p. 414.

38. David L. Featherman and Robert M. Hauser, "Sexual Inequalities and Socioeconomic Achievement in the U.S., 1962-1973," *American Sociological Review* 41 (June 1976), p. 481.

39. Blau and Hendricks, "Occupational Segregation," p. 208.

40. Blumrosen, "Wage Discrimination, Job Segregation, and Title VII," p. 412.

41. Oppenheimer, "Demographic Influence."

42. Oppenheimer, "Demographic Influence," p. 198.

43. *Dictionary of the Social Sciences.*

44. Kay Deaux and Tim Emswiller, "Explanation of Successful Performance in Sex Linked Tasks: What Is Skill for the Male Is Luck for the Female," *Journal of Personality and Social Psychology* 29, no. 1 (1974): 80-85.

45. Joan Acker, "Women and Social Stratification: A Case of Intellectual Sexism," in *Changing Woman in a Changing Society*, ed. Joan Huber (Chicago: University of Chicago Press, 1973), pp. 175-77.

46. Acker, "Women and Social Stratification," p. 178.

47. William H. Sewell, "Social Mobility and Social Participation," *Annals of the American Academy of Political and Social Sciences* (January 1978): 230-231. Also see Peter M. Blau and Otis D. Duncan, *The American Occupational Structure* (New York: John Wiley & Sons, 1967).

48. Stokely Carmichael and Charles V. Hamilton, *Black Power* (New York: Vintage Books, 1967), p. 3.

49. Amundsen, *Silenced Majority*, chap. 5. Also see Onora O'Neill, "How Do We Know When Opportunities Are Equal?" in *Sex Equality*, ed. Jane English (Englewood Cliffs, N.J.: Prentice-Hall, 1977), p. 151.

50. Elizabeth Waldman and Beverly J. McEddy, "Where Women Work: An Analysis by Industry and Occupation," *Monthly Labor Review* 97 (May 1974): 3.
51. Sandra Stencel, "Women in the Work Force," in *The Women's Movement*, Editorial Research Report, *Congressional Quarterly* (June 1977): 29.
52. Virginia Sapiro, "Equality and Preferential Treatment: A Social Psychological Perspective on Equal Employment Policies for Women," Paper presented to the European Consortium for Political Research, Florence, Italy, March 1980.
53. Amundsen, *Silenced Majority*, p. 22.
54. Amundsen, *Silenced Majority*, pp. 33, 48.
55. Pearce and McAdoo, *Women and Children*; U.S. Commission on Civil Rights, *Unemployment and Underemployment among Blacks, Hispanics, and Women*, Clearinghouse Publication 74 (November 1982).

4

Equality as Equality of Results

Equality offers more than a critique of existing inequalities. It also provides some direction as to the desirable goals and the direction necessary to achieve those goals. When properly understood, the idea of equality is a crucial ingredient of feminist analysis. The analysis, however, must be grounded in an understanding of the complexity, durability, and reinforcing dimension of existing inequalities.

Although equality has been a persistent theme in the history of political theory,[1] the term has been given a variety of meanings. Indeed almost every theorist has developed his own definition. Some have even argued that equality is a word "so wide and vague" as to be by itself almost without meaning.[2] As explained in Chapter 3, the normal functioning of the institutions of society continue to operate in a manner that creates further inequalities. If equality is not properly understood, the danger exists that the perpetuation of existing inequalities will be made in the name of equality.

The inadequacies of equality of opportunity have been evaluated.[3] However, in order to understand the importance of perceiving equality as equality of results and in properly evaluating the limitations of equality of opportunity, it is important to understand that equality of opportunity is not the only understanding of equality that is inadequate in providing feminists with a clear goal to strive towards.

The varied understandings of equality can be classified as equal consideration of interests, equality of opportunity, and equality of results.

Equality as Equal Consideration of Interest

There is a considerable body of literature that defines equality as "a denial of the propriety of making distinctions of a particular sort."[4] In other words, a claim for equality is a rejection of the legitimacy of using certain criteria, such as race or sex, in distinguishing between persons. Within this kind of definition three distinct subheads can be identified: equality as a claim against inequality, equality as treating everyone the same, and equality as impartiality.

Equality as a Claim against Inequality

The first question that must be asked is whether the feminists' claim to equality is simply a rejection of inequality based on sex. Is the demand for equality between the sexes a demand that gender no longer be considered as a valid means of choosing among persons? If so, then it might not be discriminatory to have rest rooms set aside for men and women, but it would be unequal to have a draft that would exclude women. It would also be unequal to use gender as a basis for determining hiring quotas.

There are those who explain that "the claim to human equality is never anything more than a negative egalitarianism—a limited criticism of some specific existing arrangements."[5] It would then follow that the demand for equality would not involve the requirement that all people be treated alike. Demands for equality would simply mean demands for abolition of some existing form of inequality. Thus, since social change inevitably leads to challenges to the existing way of doing business, demands for equality are no more than demands for adaptations to the new needs that changes in the society have created.[6] For example, when the Levellers urged that all Englishmen were entitled to vote, they meant only to challenge the property-owning franchise, not to extend the franchise to women or to challenge the present distribution of wealth.[7] With this kind of understanding, equality between the sexes can be reduced to arguments like "Since today the wife also must work, husbands should help with the children or take their turn cleaning the toilet bowl." This theory, of course, does not require any significant disruption of existing inequalities.[8]

Equality as Treating Everyone the Same

Part of the problem of understanding political equality is that some of the time equality means the *same*. In reapportionment decisions, for example, the concept of the equal vote means that each voter's electoral strength would be *equal* when it was the *same*. At other times it is argued that "equality is about the concept of equivalency, about x and y being equivalent to each other without necessarily being the same."[9]

Thus, racial equality between blacks and whites does not entail asking that everyone should be an identical intermediate color. Likewise, asking for equality between the sexes does not entail asking for universal hermaphroditism.[10]

Equality as treating everyone the same is said to mean that human beings should be treated in every respect in a uniform and identical manner—unless there is a sufficient reason not to do so. It must be understood, however, that this is not to imply that any one person can always claim the same treatment as any other, nor indeed that one person's interest could never have priority over another's. "Every claim must be granted on criteria specifically appropriate to it and every demand for privilege must be argued afresh," noted Isaiah Berlin. "Arguments valid in one field have no necessary consequential validity in others."[11]

This kind of argument on its face sounds so fair, so right. It is with this kind of abstract theorizing as the implicit understanding of what equality really means that we get to such nonsense terms as "reverse discrimination." This kind of equality would require that if a woman is fired for breast-feeding or for becoming pregnant, so would a man be fired. There is no questioning here of the requirements of the job or the actual work conditions. Human beings, however, are not slates that can be rubbed clean after each experience for all to begin the next endeavor. Human life is lived in very unequal societies. Inequalities are so deeply imbedded in normal human interactions that it is indeed very difficult even to conceive of what the requirements would be to treat people equally. Further, these inequalities are cumulative and reinforce each other. Thus, equality understood as treating everyone the same would certainly be a step forward—for some women. It would, however, be a step when what is needed is a mile. Further, it is unclear whether a step that is heralded as a mile does not have intrinsic in it several steps backward, that is, backlash.

Equality as Impartiality

Some argue that equality requires treating all persons alike except when there are relevant differences between them. Presume equality until there is reason to presume otherwise. When persons are treated differently, the justification for those differences must be shown. Equals should be treated equally, and unequals unequally. However, the respect in which they are considered unequal must be relevant to the proposed differences in treatment.[12] If most persons who meet certain qualifications have been given certain recognition and there are persons who have met those qualifications but have not been given the recognition, then, under this meaning of equality, the person has been treated unequally.[13] Thus, qualified women who have been excluded from receiving credit, entering graduate school, or becoming a member of the board of directors would have a claim for such rewards.

Surely many of the injustices that women now suffer could be alleviated in the name of equality as defined in these three ways. Although they do not press for the removal of all forms of differentiation, all three of these approaches to equality deny the justice of some existing modes of discrimination against women.[14] However, if feminists, in their claims for equality between the sexes, are simply asking that distinctions on the basis of sex be eliminated, the actual conditions of most women can remain very much the same or even get worse. The campaign for equal pay for women is a case in point. Advocates of these definitions of equality argue that there is no evidence that women are generally inferior to men in intelligence, business capacity, soundness of judgment, and so on. Thus, discrimination resting on such assumed inferiorities would be considered as an offense against equality. Whatever distinctions are made in any of these respects would depend on criteria applied alike to men and women. Therefore, equal pay for equal work would mean that men and women would be paid equally if and only if they work equally well. If women always worked less well than men or were less qualified, so supporters of this kind of equality assure us, then equal pay for equal work would invariably mean less pay for women. Presumably the reverse would also be true. If women always did better than men, then women would always be paid more than men. However, the criterion of differentiation would be that of excellence of performance, not gender. Again, it all sounds so desirable. To treat people according to their skill or productivity would not be considered gender discrimination even though most women might in fact receive less than men. Skill and productivity could still be claimed as the relevant and legitimate criteria—even if (or when) all the institutions operate so as to discourage such skill and productivity in women and encourage such in some men. Skill and productivity could still be claimed as the relevant and legitimate criteria—even if (or when) the skill and productivity were being evaluated exclusively by men.[15]

Equal pay for equal work would undoubtedly be an advancement in the quest for more equality for women. At least part of the reason for the discrepancy between men's and women's wages is that women frequently are paid less than men for doing the same job. However, equal pay for equal work, while a significant advancement, will do little to provide the economic conditions necessary for women to become financially equal with men.[16] An important reason for this is that while men and women are used interchangeably in some jobs, most demand for labor has been sex-specific. Women have been concentrated in occupations not only where they have been overrepresented, but where they have actually been the majority.[17] An understanding of equality as equal consideration of interests will help in the struggle for women to be paid equally with men when they do the same or similar jobs, but it would do nothing for those women who are in "women's" jobs.

Indeed advocates of equality as equal consideration of interests have cited certain "admitted biological and psychological differences between men and women" that can justify different functions in the society. The burden of proof rests on the discriminator. One such discriminator argues that discrimination according to sex for military service, or in the coal mines, can be accepted without much question. This type of discrimination can be considered well-grounded and thus not inequality.[18]

Differences in function within the family have been similarly justified. Such egalitarians can and have written that "a mother is expected to occupy herself with house and children, a father with earning the family living."[19] Further, such theorists have argued that a married woman is entitled to maintenance if her husband leaves her, but her husband does not have a corresponding right. Family allowances should be the property of mothers, but not fathers. Laws should safeguard the property rights of married women, protecting wives from the undue influence of their husband, but not conversely. It is pointed out by those who define equality as equal consideration of interest that "these distinctions are not called 'inequalities' because they are held to be justified. We call a distinction an inequality only when we have already decided to condemn it."[20]

Many feminists believe that it is this difference of function within the family that is the basis of inequality between the sexes. Juliet Mitchell writes that bearing children, bringing them up, and maintaining the home form the core of women's natural vocation in the ideology that has led to the oppression of women. Once the traditional family role is accepted, women's social subordination—however emphasized as honorable but different—can be seen to follow inevitably. "The causal chain then goes: maternity, family, absences from production and public life, sexual inequality."[21] There is more to note here than a difference of opinion on the proper familial role for women. It is also significant to notice that what feminists understand to be the very basis of inequality can be justified in the name of equality as equal consideration of interest. If the different functions in the family are to be seen as unequal, equality must be defined differently.

The consequence for defining equality as equal consideration of interest requires that advancing racial equality would necessitate the elimination of all distinctions based on race. Then persons who are black could move into expensive housing in the suburbs—if they could afford the price of the house, and find a realtor who would show them the existing holdings and a banker who would authorize the mortgage. If race is no longer a barrier to education, then all blacks might be admitted to institutions of higher education, if they meet the qualifications for acceptance.[22] If gender is no longer a determinant of being hired in a university, the women who have been evaluated as "qualified" by a large number of men throughout their training might be hired by a male, if they are considered more qualified than the men who are also applying for the position.[23] But racial equality and/or equality between the sexes would still allow the distinctions between those who could afford to pay and those who could not, those who are considered qualified and those who are not. Thus we could and certainly would have racial equality and all-white suburbs with predominantly black central cities. We could and certainly would have equality between the sexes and from 3 to 5 percent, or perhaps 10 percent, of university faculties composed of women.

The problem with this kind of definition is that it defines equality according to one rule. It is presumed that whenever we treat according to a rule, we will be treating equally. Clearly, then, the crucial question becomes "according to what rule should we treat people in this case?" Such an analysis of equality cannot answer this question because it requires that we choose between inequalities. We will rarely, if ever, be able to treat equally in one respect without treating unequally in others.[24] Thus, this definition of equality requires using criteria other than equality to choose between competing equalities. The job of fem-

Equality of Opportunity

Equality of opportunity asserts that each person should have equal rights and opportunities to develop her or his own talents and virtues and that there should be equal rewards for equal performance. Some have argued that equality of opportunity is simply the substitution of reasonable for objectionable distinctions and that, therefore, equality of opportunity is simply another name for equality as equal consideration of interest.[25] Equality of opportunity, however, does differ from equal consideration of interest. With equality of opportunity there is a strong presumption that there has been discrimination in the past and that something "different" must be done in the future. The person who presses for equality of opportunity is urging that certain characteristics that in the past determined the extent of an individual's opportunities, such as wealth, race, or sex, should no longer be factors in determining a person's opportunities. The claim is made that something must be done to allow all people to maximize their abilities to their fullest. The primary intention is to give the qualified persons who have experienced discrimination the chance to show their capabilities. Again, there is no attempt here to minimize inequalities among people. Inequalities would continue. Indeed, they might increase. Equality of opportunity simply requires that those who are qualified receive the rewards that are due to them. Additionally, no one would be excluded from gaining the qualifications.[26] There is no guarantee for those who are not qualified—except the certainty that they will receive less of society's rewards than the qualified. There is no attempt here to revise the rules of the game. Equality of opportunity would simply require that the rules be made more fair in that they be applied in the same way to everyone.[27]

One problem with equality of opportunity, as John Schaar has pointed out, is that not all talents can be developed equally in any given society. "Out of the great variety of human resources available to it, a given society will admire and reward some abilities more than others."[28] Any person who is concerned with making a significant dent in the inequalities that now exist on the basis of gender must take into consideration the characteristics that are encouraged in women and the value that those talents now have in contemporary society. Boys are trained to be independent in action, to dominate others, and to be able to control their emotions. They are encouraged to be aggressive and to seek intellectual excellence. On the other hand, girls are encouraged to be dependent and passive and to conform. They are discouraged from being aggressive or too intellectual.[29] Kirsten Amundsen asserts that "society's dictations of what is desirable in a female child preclude the development of independence of mind, intellectual inquisitiveness and a drive to compete."[30]

Instead, most women have been trained to seek their fulfillment through personal relationships.[31] Shulamith Firestone is most critical of this emphasis in the training of girls. She particularly criticizes romantic love between men and women. According to her, "love is the pivot of women's oppression today."[32] She argues that relationships between men and women are necessarily relationships between unequals. These inequalities make it impossible to have a personal relationship that is not harmful to the less powerful person. She is also critical of romantic love because it encourages women to occupy themselves with personal relationships rather than with issues of public concern. "Women live for love and men for work." "Women are not creating cultures because they are preoccupied with love."[33]

Neither Firestone nor other feminists are advocating that girls be totally socialized into accepting male values. It is indeed quite frightening to think of associations between men and women, or any other relationships in a society, where personal relationships had little to no value. Nor are feminists advocating that only feminine values should exist and/or predominate. They see problems with feminine values as well. The point here, however, is to realize that implicit in an equal-opportunity concept of equality is the acceptance of the present value structure. Currently most girls and women are socialized away from the kind of characteristics that are valued highly in the general society. Further, they are conditioned to accept values that the contemporary society ignores and/or finds suspicious and, in fact, often penalizes. Women may not be admitted to graduate schools or professional schools because they will leave to get married or to have a baby. Women may not be given the promotion because they will not move without their family. And if they do not behave as anticipated, then something is wrong with them and they should not get admitted to the program or be given the promotion.

Thus in understanding the concept of equality of opportunity we must understand which values receive which rewards in the society and the significance of that for all citizens. As John Schaar pointed out, persons who strive to develop potentialities that are not admired in a given society face sanctions or are certainly hampered in their efforts to achieve the society's rewards. Moreover, every society encourages some talents and discourages others. Equality of opportunity allows all to develop those talents that are highly valued by a given society in a given time.[34] "There is . . . a hierarchy of values even among those talents, virtues and contests that are encouraged: the winners in some contests are rewarded more handsomely than the winners in other contests."[35]

Feminists understand this but often do not see the implications for a society that would guarantee equality of opportunity for women. Kirsten Amundsen explains that feminine virtues are praised by those who would use the existence of these virtues to keep women in a secondary status: "On the basis of the knowledge that she is less intellectually assertive, less ambitious, and more emotional than men, that she has less superego and therefore weaker social interests, one can with great ease assign her to the traditional roles and to the place she was always accustomed to behind the man."[36]

Aware of the previous discrimination involved in treating people differently in order to exclude them, advocates of equality of opportunity assume that rules applied similarly will be applied equally. However, to apply the same rule when the circumstances are not equivalent provides no guarantee of equality. The "justice" of a legal system that equally fines a rich man or a poor man for sleeping under a bridge is readily apparent. Likewise, an employer who fires a woman or man who becomes pregnant provides another clear example of the problem. Less clear, but similarly absurd, attempts to neutralize sex as the basis for decision-making occur regularly. Personnel screening committees look for letters of recommendation that sound as good from women candidates as from their male competitors. Meanwhile, graduate professors try hard to "keep their distance" from female graduate students.

Feminists repeatedly explain how society has encouraged women to reject "the development of independence of mind, intellectual inquisitiveness, assertiveness and a drive to compete." They are encouraged instead to be "nice" and, above all, to *find a man*. At the same time, equality of opportunity is stressed in the educational institutions. Women are encouraged to be agreeable and then are not given as high a grade because they are not aggressive enough. They are encouraged "not to sound too smart" and then are not allowed into doctoral programs because they are "not serious enough." Educational institutions that treat men and women equally evaluate women by the same standards as men and more often than not find the women less competent. The results are not more equality in education for women, but simply more evidence for women that they indeed deserve to receive less from the society—for, indeed, they are less. They had their chances but they were not quite tough enough.[37]

There are, of course, women for whom rules applied equally would mean significant advancement. Often it is these women who articulate the problems concerning existing inequalities on the basis of gender. Furthermore, it is difficult in this society to ask for any considerations other than those on merit. Although little in fact is based primarily on merit, the existing myths demand that all decisions be justified in its name. Even the most qualified of women have been made aware of their limitations. After all, they are women. It is indeed difficult for persons who are always aware of that limitation to attack such a powerful existing myth as "merit." Nonetheless, this argument must be made if any movement toward more equality is to be achieved.[38]

Rules that are applied similarly in different situations cannot ensure equality. With perhaps the exception of differences in social class, women more than any other group make this case most dramatically. Catholics and Protestants in Northern Ireland "might" both give up their faith and live together happily ever after. Blacks and whites in the United States "might" intermarry. The French and English in Canada "might" all learn a third language. It is, however, difficult to conceive of a society in which differences in sex are completely eliminated. Thus, the "woman's question" requires confronting the issue of how differences are dealt with equally. In such a stratified society, similar treatment is inherently unequal treatment. In attempting to create a society in which equality of opportunity could work, John Rawls resorted to a hypothetical position.[39] In this original position, inequalities are eliminated and people start off the same. If we wish to achieve more equality, though, I suspect it is more realistic to revise our concept of equality than it is to try to get to the original position. Inequalities exist and the understanding of equality as equality of opportunity justifies the perpetuation of those inequalities.

Thus how equal are opportunities when the rules are applied uniformly yet certain groups have been excluded from making the rules, and/or when those excluded groups dispute the rules by which the "game" is being played?[40] In their demands for equality, feminists must reject many of the values implicit in the status quo. These values are rejected because they are impossible to maintain in a society that practices equality between the sexes,[41] or because they are undesirable. Some feminists have asked for child-care facilities and maternity leaves in the name of equality of opportunity.[42] Feminists argue that equality is achieved only when appropriate proportions of jobs at all levels are held by workers who are women and/or members of minority groups. If this is not the case, there must be evidence of serious attempts to recruit and promote members of the underrepresented group.[43] Equality of opportunity is simply not adequate to justify demands of this nature. The primary problem with equality of opportunity is not what it does but rather what it does not do. The main limitation of equality of opportunity is that it does not direct attention to the outcomes of public policies. Feminists try to ask for significant changes in the status quo in the name of equality of opportunity. I am convinced, however, that no particular changes, in themselves, are adequate to meet the goals feminists wish to achieve. Any procedures can be manipulated to maintain inequalities. Inequalities involve power, and the powerful usually work to maintain their power. Furthermore, they are usually successful. It is important to realize that the existing pattern of values has kept women at the bottom of the system. If the total pattern is not challenged, only a few "superwomen"—judged superwomen by male values, if not exclusively by men—will squeak through. For most members of any exploited group, however, equality will mean little except a justification for their unequal position. The only way to ameliorate inequalities in such an unequal world—that is, the only way to achieve more equality—will be based on our ability to evaluate the outcomes of any public policies and to make the moral claim that equality requires minimizing the differences among persons. We need different rules. Furthermore, we need to be aware of the ends we wish to achieve and continually evaluate the rules to see how well they accomplish those ends. It must be presumed that the normal functioning of the social institutions work to maintain and perpetuate inequalities. The rules we adopt to modify those inequalities must continually be evaluated with that knowledge in mind.

Such an analysis does not, of course, guarantee more equality. However, if we do not look at the outcomes, continued and perhaps greater inequalities are to be expected. No doubt some of the inequalities will be perpetuated in the name of equality.[44]

Equality of Results

The terms sexual equality, equality between the sexes, or equality of gender are used regularly in feminist literature. Quite often, however, equality is applied without any analysis of its meaning. Or it is defined in one sentence and then applied, or the definition that is used is not appropriate for the analysis that follows.[45] Whether they are aware of it or not, the only definition of equality that can meet the feminists' demands is equality of results. The only understanding of equality that can be adequately applied to programs that will lessen inequality between the sexes is equality of results.

Equality of results presupposes that equality is not merely the equal consideration of interests, nor simply the absence of social impediments based on sex to any individual's attaining whatever position in society for which she or he chooses to aim. Instead, for groups that have suffered severe discrimination, a demand for equality requires significant social changes in order to achieve a society that guarantees a certain level of physical and economic security for all members.[46] Those at the bottom of the social structure must ask for raising the bottom and decreasing the discrepancy between those who have and those who do not have. Otherwise, all but a few (possibly exceptional) persons will stay at the bottom.

The justification for this conception of equality is its affirmation of equality of being or belonging.[47] People are valued as ends in themselves. We recognize something that is highly and equally valuable in all persons but has nothing to do with their merit. It is this recognition that constitutes the claim for equal rights.[48] Thus all persons are to be treated as equals not because they are equal in any particular respect, but simply because they are human.[49] This assertion is absolutely essential if we are to break the cycle of inequality. If we do not make such an assertion and fail to work toward that reality, inequalities are perpetuated and possibly intensified. Such assertions are more than noble statements; they are the only hope that any society has for making significant steps toward greater equality.

One major advantage of equality of results is that implicit in the definition is the understanding that equal concern for the good lives of its members requires a society to treat people differently. Individual experiences, needs, capacities, and interests differ, and what constitutes the good life for one individual may not do so for another. Human beings have never been treated the same. However, equality of results differs from "business as usual" in that it argues that it is society's very concern for the good life of its members that determines which differences and which similarities it must respect. The norm used is the equal participation of all in the life of the community. The only way in which all citizens will be able to participate equally is if they are treated differently. The decision on how to treat people is made by looking at the consequences of different policies for them and evaluating those policies in light of how they contribute to the equal participation in the life of the community of all its members. Because people are not the same, policies are adopted that treat people differently in order to treat them equally. But they are treated differently because they should be treated equally well.[50]

A second advantage of equality of results is that it is the only understanding of equality that emphasizes similarities among persons and minimizes differences. The feminist conception of political equality involves a society in which gender is no longer used to discriminate against anybody in public life. Regardless of the magnitude of the change this may entail, however, feminists ask for much more. If all the feminist concerns involved were a society in which discrimination on the basis of sex was abolished, then most women perhaps would not be quite as unequal as they are today. They would, nonetheless, be unequal—as unequal as their husbands, fathers, brothers, or lovers. Perhaps even a few women would have their status significantly improved, but there is certainly a large question whether that is tactically possible. Without some significant redistribution of resources, how is it possible to eliminate or even lessen the discrimination against one group?

It is, of course, extremely difficult to discuss equality for any one group in such an unequal world. Could some women be raised to greater economic parity only to be replaced in the lower economic strata by men? While quite unlikely, it might be possible. It would not, however, meet feminist demands. Greater equality must involve more rights for everybody to what is necessary for the good life. No matter what the cleavages along traditional lines—for example, socialist or nonsocialist,

Marxist or non-Marxist, liberal or radical—feminists want more than a society that guarantees to everybody similar rights to be unequal. Feminists most specifically ask for a society in which there is a considerable reduction in all existing inequalities.[51]

What would it mean if there were to be no differences among people? Such a question is enormously complex. Much has been written on the subject, but not by feminists.[52] While this is certainly a criticism of feminist literature, it must be seen in perspective. In a practical sense, feminists are painfully aware that revolutions won in the name of equality have not improved the condition of women.[53] There is some suggestion that, in fact, they have made the inequalities on the basis of gender even greater. On a theoretical level, it is important to realize that every issue cannot be dealt with at the same time. The issue that is specifically the women's question has not been adequately given serious consideration in the ongoing male discussions on inequality any more than women's rights have been recognized in male-dominated social movements for equality. To deal thoroughly with the other issues of inequality might well take the attention away again from the issue of inequality on the basis of gender. Discussions of women's role in the family and/or the economy can and have been brushed aside as trivial while the emphasis is put on how to redistribute income.

Feminists must recognize that differences in equalities on the basis of gender are not the only inequalities that exist or are significant. Juliet Mitchell warns that if we simply develop feminist consciousness, we will not get political consciousness but a kind of chauvinism. She warns against a perspective that sees only the oppression of one's own group.[54] Nonetheless, which inequalities seem the greatest—race, sex, or class— depends on a person's race, sex, or class. Furthermore, those most appropriate to discuss inequalities are those most affected by them. Because they are feminist and come to their understanding of equality and inequality on the basis of their experience with inequalities of gender, it is most appropriate that it is those inequalities that feminists emphasize. This emphasis does not mean to exclude other kinds of inequalities. It simply requires that due attention be given to gender inequalities. When they ask for equality, feminists are asking for a reduction of the differences between persons on the basis of gender. They are asking for equality of results.

The results to be achieved are not absolute equality of condition, but enough equality of condition to allow more equal participation in citizenship for women. This understanding of equality recognizes the fact that more equality in the economic and other institutions is a necessary but not a sufficient condition for democracy. It also recognizes that there must be changes in the existing social institutions that reinforce oppressed peoples' acceptance of their secondary status. Furthermore, it takes into consideration the fact that these changes that are absolutely necessary are also very difficult to achieve. Any of the policies that seem to be useful toward reaching those goals might be meaningless or even counterproductive. The only check on that possibility is constant awareness of the goals and constant evaluation of the policies. The aim is "a society in which no person should be so powerless that she or he has no control whatsoever over his or her own life; a society in which no person should be so powerful that he or she can force others to do her or his bidding without taking others into acccunt";[55] a society in which all those virtually affected by a decision of the community have an effective voice in that decision.[56] Any understanding of equality that aims for less may well be clever manipulation of logic and language, but it is indeed something other than equality!

Another advantage of equality of results is that it directs us to look at the outcomes. Policies are evaluated to the extent that they help reach the desired outcomes. Inequalities are so deeply entrenched in society that it is essential that any definition of equality must be similarly pervasive. Such an assumption provides a major contribution of feminists to an understanding of equality. No matter how sensible, desirable, or functional any one program sounds, it is more than likely that because of rigidity of the inequalities and/or because of the opposition to change, the program will not always make for greater equality. While an understanding of equality as equality of results will not avoid that problem, it can compensate for it by asking those concerned with equality to look to what the program accomplishes and to avoid excessive commitment to any one program.

Persons who are less than equal have fewer options in manipulating the laws, norms, and symbols of the society to their advantage.[57] Any movement for more equality must be constantly aware of that problem. For example, there have been endless, futile discussions over the issue of busing school children for purposes of racial integration. Although the arguments have been made, it is difficult to be for or against "the principle" of children riding a bus. The desired result is equal education for all children regardless of race and/or social class. Within that framework, because of the existing segregation of housing patterns, it may sometimes be necessary to bus in order to achieve that end. Certainly, integrated housing is a more important component among the factors necessary to achieve the goal. And even more certainly, busing within city limits will only create more inequalities. For those points to be seen, however, the goals to be achieved must be the focus of the discussion. Once the focus is on the issue of busing or affirmative action, given the existing inequalities in the society and how they translate into greater power, influence, and communication skills, the failure of any of these programs to lessen inequalities can be virtually guaranteed. That focus is simply too narrow.

To illustrate the problem of reducing equality to such a narrow focus, two examples will be considered: affirmative action, or preferential treatment, and no-fault divorce.

Affirmative Action

Affirmative action requires an employer or educational institution to tip evenly balanced scales in favor of a candidate from an underrepresented group. If two persons are similarly qualified, affirmative action requires that the candidate from the underrepresented group should be hired or admitted. Preferential hiring and quota admissions, on the other hand, are stronger programs. The employer or educational institution must use different criteria in accepting persons from underrepresented groups.

It is not the purpose of this section to argue that we must develop the concept of equality of results in order to justify affirmative action or preferential treatment. Indeed, theorists have justified affirmative action and preferential treatment by understanding equality as equal consideration of interests,[58] and equality of opportunity.[59] The intention here is to show how affirmative action or preferential treatment needs to be evaluated in a larger perspective that does not favor preferential treatment but favors equality—equality of results.

The different treatment involved in affirmative action or preferential treatment are necessary for three primary reasons: (1) a person's own sense (real or imagined) of his or her inadequacies significantly limit his or her opportunities; (2) even when two persons are equally qualified, the person who makes the choices, because of discrimination, may believe that the oppressed person is less qualified; and (3) the nature of the qualifications required might not adequately reflect the job to be filled.[60]

The actual attainment of qualifications is not a neutral process. Access to proper qualifications, confidence that one is capable of doing the job, and confidence that qualifications will make a difference are also gender-related. If all the support from family, teachers, selection committees, grant committees, fellow students, and so on, are provided for boys and men and not for girls and women, then it is indeed more likely that the man will be more qualified. Furthermore, whether or not the man is more qualified, it is more likely that everyone, including the person being evaluated, will consider men more qualified than women.[61]

It is important to remember that attempts to create more equality or less inequality are not being made in isolation.[62] If women are to be chosen for promotions, admission to schools, etc., the judgments will be made primarily by men. And if not by men, then by women who have been socialized in a sexist society. "Recent research demonstrates conclusively that prejudice and stereotype still serve to depress evaluations of women, and on the part of both men and women," notes Virginia Sapiro. "The issue is whether women face, at every stage at which evaluation has an effect on their careers, the obstacle of non-conscious discrimination against them. Experimental research by psychologists suggest they do."[63]

One of the most fallacious arguments about "reverse discrimination" is the threat that somehow we will be choosing the less-qualified person—as if there is some clearly defined understanding of what it means to be qualified. The uncertainty of proper qualifications is most obvious in admissions to universities and professional schools. Long before the issue of affirmative action or preferential treatment arose, qualifications varied from school to school. John would get into Yale University Law School and be turned down at the University of Chicago Law School. Meanwhile Bob would get into Chicago but be turned down by Yale. It was understood that schools in their search for proper qualifications considered geographic balance and some balance in "other factors." The thought was that more varied student backgrounds would provide a better educational environment for all students.

There are two separate issues involved in the consideration of proper qualification for admission to universities and professional schools: the educational environment created by the students admitted and the job the graduate will hold after graduation. In both cases it seems reasonable to suppose that race and sex should be considered as valid factors in achieving both goals.[64]

For reasons that go beyond the issue of sexism, it is essential to question the present understanding of qualifications. As I see students scrambling to get into veterinary school, the evaluations traditionally used to single out the most qualified students do not identify the kinds of people that I would want to treat *my* dogs or cats. Is the score on one or several organic chemistry courses a better determiner than sex of the capacity to consider advances in reproductive medicine, or a better determiner than race of qualification to work on curing sickle cell anemia? Problems of adequate qualifications are not just a problem for admissions to schools. They are problems that haunt every aspect of the evaluative process in our credential-crazy world. People usually considered the most qualified scholars and/or teachers have the hardest time getting published, getting tenure, getting grants or other gold stars. There is no doubt that these observations in academia hold true in other areas of employment as well.

One of the most dangerous tendencies among academic feminists is the danger of wishing to appear as qualified as the men who are judging them. No doubt that feminists who have been able to achieve some success in other areas have similar tendencies. It is, of course, understandable that they should strive to do so—but dangerous, nonetheless. First of all, it is impossible. As long as the judges are overwhelmingly male and there are only a few "exceptional" women, there is no way ever that a woman will be evaluated as just another colleague, doctor, lawyer, teacher. Sometimes a woman's qualifications or talents may be inflated: "She's good—even if she is a woman." But in that judgment there is a hidden suspicion. Is she womanly enough? If not, then she does not quite exist. And if she is, then she is not quite qualified.[65]

The question of qualifications must also be challenged because, except for a few tokens, most women will be continually discriminated against unless the qualifications are changed.[66] The pressures and tensions are simply too great to expect that most women can put up with the costs involved in attempting achievements in the "male," that is, the real, world. There will be no equality for women in public life unless there are many women in positions of authority, status, and influence. If women are to attain these positions, then qualifications must be re-examined.[67]

Further, the qualifications are not working to get the most qualified people. Medical schools are not producing doctors that deal well with women and/or minorities—and not really all that well with most white men. Political science does not produce the kinds of scholars who can analyze the issues of inequality on the basis of race or the problems of the inner cities. The auto industry and other industrial plants are not hiring people who produce quality products. It is not accidental that we have poor scholarship, poor medicine, and inferior products. It is built into the nature of the kinds of qualifications that are used. Most of the time the qualifications are simply not appropriate to the job that needs to be done.[68] That is, of course, a much larger issue than can be dealt with satisfactorily here. The main point to be made is that feminists must and can attack the whole definition of qualifications if any progress toward equality between the sexes or among persons in general is to be made. Furthermore, those qualifications are open to a great deal of criticism.

Such an attack should include the relevance of sex and race to adequate qualifications to do the job. For example, black police who are well trained can make the inner cities safer, black teachers who are qualified will be more capable of teaching black and white students how to read and how to live in a racially integrated world, and men and women students will be better served by knowing female as well as male college professors. Feminine traits can lead to better scholarship, better teaching, and better collegial relations. Affirmative action can lead to better, not perfect, scholars, doctors, and lawyers.[69] Race and sex are certainly not sufficient qualifications for jobs, but because of the sexist and racist nature of society, they are often significant variables *in themselves* that should be taken into consideration in the efforts to find the most qualified person to do the job that needs to be done.

While essential and useful in lessening the sexism in society, programs of preferential treatment cannot become goals in themselves. A recent study of the court-ordered affirmative action program at American Telephone and Telegraph illustrates the importance of keeping the focus on the end result. The court decision in that case was a landmark for feminists. The implementation of the program, however, provided little comfort to those concerned with equality between the sexes. In this case the researcher found more white men were hired into traditionally female jobs than minorities and/or women were hired in jobs that had been previously held by white men; the jobs that were made available to minorities and women primarily were being slowly phased out because of technological advancements; and when white men were asked, their overwhelming consensus was that, because of affirmative action, it was impossible for a white man to be hired at AT&T![70]

Equality of Results and No-Fault Divorce

Feminist theory clearly demonstrates the relevance of family structures to the issue of equal citizenship for women. Indeed, there is considerable controversy about the relationship between equality between the sexes and women's role in the family.[71] No matter what is perceived as the ideal familial role for women, however, the question of divorce will not go away. Divorce is an increasing possibility that all married persons must face.

Within the past fifteen years, divorce law has changed considerably in the United States by means of a reform called no-fault divorce. No-fault divorce eliminates the need to prove legal "fault" to dissolve a marriage and eliminates punitive financial settlements to "punish" guilty partners.[72] It would be difficult for anyone committed to social justice and reform to advocate the adversary relationship in the divorce courts. As in the case of affirmative action, if equality is not seen as equality of results, the reform involved in no-fault divorce will simply provide a new way in which existing inequalities will be perpetuated in the name of equality.

The well-intentioned judge in a divorce case can now rest easy when he grants middle-age, middle-class women divorces without alimony—all in the name of equality. These women are then "free," often to work for the minimum wage! If they are given the added opportunity of meeting the mortgage payment, how are they to do that on the salary of a store clerk? Are they to be blamed for being "unqualified"? In a sexist society, in which all qualifications have at least the taint of sexism, what does it mean to be "qualified" for a living wage as a woman? (The notion of what a living wage is might be open to interesting speculation. That most women make less than a living wage is so far beyond refutation that it would not fit into such interesting speculation.) The kind of analysis that would call the decision of a judge, who dealt with both persons the same, as equal will be used to perpetuate various types of exploitation of women—and of other disadvantaged persons.[73]

This was precisely the conclusion that was made in a study of no-fault divorce in California. No-fault divorce went into effect in California as a result of the Family Law Act on January 1, 1970. Judges in California have implemented no-fault divorce in a manner that is called equal. They often split all assets into two equal parts. This usually requires that the family home must be sold. The children, however, are still usually awarded to the mother. As this study clearly shows, the result of no-fault divorce has been to put women into an even worse financial situation than they were in previously. They are forced to sell their house but do not have the financial status to buy another one. They receive less in child-support payments and are required to pay expensive child-care services. All this has been done in the name of reform, in the name of equality.[74] "The introduction of no-fault divorce legislation in California was not opposed by women in general or by feminist groups in particular, although adverse impact might have been predicted from the law's provisions that assets be equally divided regardless of circumstances," noted Karen Seal. *"The belief in equality is so fundamental, however, that arguing for more than an equal divison of assets, or income for women, could be interpreted as discrimination against men."*[75]

Indeed, women did not do well in the divorce courts previously. They did even worse in attempting to get the financial settlements, especially child-support payments, enforced by the courts. No-fault divorce makes a difficult situation for women even worse.[76]

On a theoretical level again, no-fault divorce sounds so reasonable, so fair, so equal. In actual operation, it provides another illustration of the way in which treating people the same when the conditions are very different perpetuates inequality. The only meaning of equality that will facilitate the eradication of gender as a limitation on the life chances for women is equality perceived as equality of results.[77]

In summary, feminists are asking to minimize the differences between all people. They recognize that differences in equalities on the basis of gender are not the only inequalities that exist or that are significant. Because they are feminist and come to their understanding of equality and inequality on the basis of their experience with inequalities of gender, it is most appropriate that it is those inequalities that feminists emphasize. This emphasis does not mean to exclude other kinds of inequalities. It simply requires that due attention be given to gender inequalities. When they ask for equality, they must demand equality of results.

Notes

1. J. Roland Pennock and John W. Chapman, eds., *Nomos IX: Equality* (New York: Atherton Press, 1967), p. ix.
2. Hugo Adam Bedau, "Egalitarianism and the Idea of Equality," in Pennock and Chapman, *Nomos IX*, p. 4; and Bernard Williams, "The Idea of Equality," in *Philosophy, Politics, and Society*, ed. Peter Laslett and W. G. Runciman (London: Oxford University Press, 1962), p. 111.
3. Daniel Maguire, *A New American Justice* (Garden City, N.Y.: Doubleday and Company, 1980); Lawrence B. Joseph, "Some Ways of Thinking about Equality of Opportunity," *Western Political Quarterly* 33 (September 1980): 393-400.
4. S. I. Benn and R. S. Peters, *The Principles of Political Thought* (New York: The Free Press, 1959), p. 145.
5. George E. G. Catlin, "Equality and What We Mean by It," in Pennock and Chapman, *Nomos IX*, p. 104.
6. John Plamenatz, "Diversity of Rights and Kinds of Equality," in Pennock and Chapman, *Nomos IX*, pp. 83-84.
7. Benn and Peters, *Principles*, p. 132.
8. For example, one study of equality as a claim against inequality suggests that "Nevertheless, this does not justify elevating the husband into a lord and master—nor the complete sacrifice of the woman's personality to the demands of the family. Many husbands now recognize that the domestic burden carried by mothers of families in previous generations was out of all proportion to the difference in function implied by the difference in sex. The readiness to share the chores and the baby minding has been cited as a sign of the practical extension of the principle of equal consideration," Benn and Peters, *Principles*, p. 136.
9. Robert Booth Fowler and Jeffery R. Orenstein, *Contemporary Issues in Political Theory* (New York: John Wiley & Sons, 1977), p. 76.
10. Brian Barry, *Political Argument* (New York: Humanities Press, 1965), p. 120.
11. Isaiah Berlin, "Equality as an Ideal," in *Justice and Social Policy*, ed. Frederick A. Olafson (Englewood Cliffs, N.J.: Prentice-Hall, 1961), p. 129.
12. Benn and Peters, *Principles*, pp. 127-128.
13. Plamenatz, "Diversity," p. 85.
14. Barry, *Political Argument*, p. 65.
15. Barry, *Political Argument*, p. 65; and Benn and Peters, *Principles*, p. 135.
16. Gary D. Brown, "Discrimination and Pay Disparities between White Men and Women," *Monthly Labor Review* 101 (March 1978): 22; Ruth G. Blumrosen, "Wage Discrimination, Job Segregation, and Title VII of the Civil

Rights Act of 1964," *University of Michigan Journal of Law Reform* 12 (Spring 1979): 476.

17. Deborah Bachrach, "Women in Employment," *Clearinghouse Review/ National Clearinghouse for Legal Services* 14 (February 1981): 1041.
18. Barry, *Political Argument*, p. 65; Benn and Peters, *Principles*, p. 135.
19. Benn and Peters, *Principles*, p. 136.
20. Benn and Peters, *Principles*, p. 136.
21. Juliet Mitchell, *Women's Estate* (New York: Vintage Books, 1970), p. 107.
22. Barry, *Political Argument*, p. 123.
23. Virginia Sapiro, "Equality and 'Preferential Treatment': A Social Psychological Perspective on Equal Employment Policies for Women," presented at the European Consortium for Political Research, Florence, Italy, March 1980.
24. "Consider the following hypothetical case: school districts A and B would both benefit from receiving X dollars of state aid. State resources are sufficiently great to give to A and B without hampering other programs. A, however, has a large population of educationally deprived children and B does not. It would be right to give X to both A and B, and to give X to A and not to B would be to treat them unequally in one important respect. It has been argued, however, that to do the latter would not be wrong. The inequality would not lead to bad results for B and hence it would be based upon a permissible classification," Richard E. Flatham, "Equality and Generalization: A Formal Analysis," in Pennock and Chapman, *Nomos IX*, p. 50.
25. Benn and Peters, *Principles*, p. 138.
26. Alice Rossi, "Sex Equality: The Beginning of an Ideology," in *Masculine/Feminine: Readings in Sexual Mythology and the Liberation of Women*, ed. Betty and Theodore Roszak (New York: Harper Colophon Books, 1969), p. 176.
27. Jean Bethke Elshtain, "The Feminist Movement and the Question of Equality," *Polity* 7, no. 4 (Summer 1975): 471.
28. John H. Schaar "Equality of Opportunity, and Beyond," in Pennock and Chapman, *Nomos IX*, p. 236.
29. Kirsten Amundsen, *A New Look at the Silenced Majority: Women and American Democracy* (Englewood Cliffs, N.J.: Prentice-Hall, 1977), p. 107. See also, Beverly Blair Cook, "Sex Roles and the Burger Court," *American Politics Quarterly* 5 (July 1977): 353-394; Karen S. Cook and Richard M. Emerson, "Power, Equity, and Commitment in Exchange Networks," *American Sociological Review* 43 (October 1978): 721-739; Janet Lever, "Sex Differences in the Complexity of Children's Play and Games," *American Sociological Review* 43 (August 1978): 471-482.
30. Amundsen, *Silenced Majority*, p. 108.
31. Jo Freeman, *The Politics of Women's Liberation* (New York: David

McKay Company, 1975), p. 141. See also Elizabeth Janeway, *Powers of the Weak* (New York: Alfred A. Knopf, 1980).

32. Shulamith Firestone, *The Dialectic of Sex: The Case for Feminist Revolution* (New York: Bantam Books, 1970), p. 126.

33. Firestone, *Dialectic of Sex*, p. 127.

34. Firestone, *Dialectic of Sex*, pp. 132-133.

35. Schaar, "Equality of Opportunity," p. 236; Michael Walzer, "In Defense of Equality," *Dissent* 20 (Fall 1973).

36. Amundsen, *Silenced Majority*, pp. 101, 106; Irene Diamond, *Sex Roles in the State House* (New Haven, Conn.: Yale University Press, 1977); Carolyn P. Edwards and Beatrice B. Whiting, "Women and Dependency," *Politics and Society* 4, no. 3 (1974).

37. Amundsen, *Silenced Majority*, p. 111.

38. Elshtain, "Feminist Movement," p. 461; Sapiro, "Equality and 'Preferential Treatment.' "

39. John Rawls, *A Theory of Justice* (Cambridge: Harvard University Press, Belknap Press, 1971).

40. For instance, "many feminists are critical of the criteria used to assess academic productivity," says Alice Rossi. "They ask that the quality of teaching, the degree of colleagueship with students, the extent of service to both an academic institution and its surrounding community become part of the criteria on which productivity of an academic man or woman is evaluated." See Rossi, "Sex Equality," p. 184.

41. For example, Alice Rossi notes that "life in the top strata of business and professional occupations . . . has been possible only because . . . wives were leading traditional lives as homemakers, doing double parent and household duty, and carrying the major burden of civic responsibilities. If it were not for their wives in the background, successful men in American society would have to be single or childless. This is why so many professional women complain . . . that what they most need . . . is a 'wife'." See Rossi, "Sex Equality," p. 183.

42. Mary C. Segers, "Equality, Public Policy, and Relevant Sex Differences," *Polity* 2 (1979): 319-339.

43. Onora O'Neill, "How Do We Know When Opportunities Are Equal?" in *Sexual Equality*, ed. Jane English (Englewood Cliffs, N.J.: Prentice-Hall, 1977), p. 148.

44. Elshtain, "Feminist Movement," p. 471.

45. See, for example, Alison Jagger, "On Sexual Equality," in English, *Sex Equality*. Also see O'Neill, "How Do We Know," Rossi, "Sex Equality," and Segers, "Equality, Public Policy and Relevant Sex Differences." All four of these articles are most useful for understanding equality between the sexes. I believe, however, that all four approaches would fit more appropriately under an analysis of equality of results.

46. Herbert Gans, *More Equality* (New York: Vintage Books, 1973), p. iv.
47. Schaar, "Equality of Opportunity," p. 247.
48. Schaar, "Equality of Opportunity," p. 247. Also see Elshtain, "Feminist Movement."
49. William K. Frankena, "The Concept of Social Justice," in *Social Justice*, ed. Richard B. Brandt (Englewood Cliffs, N.J.: Prentice-Hall, 1962), p. 19.
50. "It is what justifies, for example, giving C a banjo, D a guitar, and E a skin-diving outfit," notes William Frankena. "Although C, D, and E are created differently, they are not dealt with unequally, since their differing needs and capacities so far as these relate to the good life are equally considered and equally well cared for." Frankena, "Concept of Social Justice," p. 20.
51. Zillah Eisenstein, *The Radical Future of Liberal Feminism* (New York: Longman, 1981), p. 231.
52. Robert A. Dahl, "On Removing Certain Impediments to Democracy in the United States," *Dissent* 25 (Summer 1978); Gans, *More Equality*; R. H. Tawney, *Equality* (New York: Harcourt Brace & Company, 1929); Walzer, "In Defense of Equality"; Michael Young, "Is Equality a Dream?" *Dissent* 20 (Fall 1973). For a feminist approach, see Marge Piercy, *Woman on the Edge of Time* (New York: Fawcett Crest Books, 1976).
53. Mitchell, *Women's Estate*, p. 122.
54. Mitchell, *Women's Estate*, p. 96.
55. Gans, *More Equality*, p. 10.
56. C. W. Mills, *The Sociological Imagination* (London: Oxford University Press, 1959).
57. Donald C. Baumer, Carl E. Van Horn, and Mary Marvel, "Explaining Benefit Distribution in CETA Programs," *Journal of Human Resources* 14, no. 2.
58. S. I. Benn, "Egalitarianism and the Equal Consideration of Interest," in Pennock and Chapman, *Nomos IX*, p. 75.
59. O'Neill, "How Do We Know," pp. 152-153.
60. Elliot M. Zashin, "Affirmative Action and Federal Personnel Systems," *Public Policy* 28, no. 3 (Summer 1980): 351-380.
61. Kay Deaux and Tim Emswiller, "Explanations of Successful Performance in Sex-Linked Tasks: What Is Skill for the Male Is Luck for the Female," *Journal of Personality and Social Psychology* 29, no. 1 (1974): 80-85. Also, Blumrosen, "Wage Discrimination, Job Segregation, and Title VII," pp. 434-448.
62. Barbara F. Reskin, "Sex Differences in Status Attainment in Science: The Case of the Postdoctoral Fellowship," *American Sociological Review* 41 (August 1976): 597-612; Marjorie Randon Hershey, "The Politics of Androgyny? Sex Roles and Attitudes toward Women in Politics." *American Politics Quarterly* 5 (July 1977): 261-287.

63. Sapiro, "Equality and 'Preferential Treatment.' "
64. U.S. Commission on Civil Rights, *Toward Equal Educational Opportunity: Affirmative Admissions Programs at Law and Medical School*, Clearinghouse Publication 55 (June 1978).
65. Marianne A. Ferber, Jane W. Loeb, and Helen M. Lowry, "The Economic Status of Women Faculty: A Reappraisal," *Journal of Human Resources* 13 (Summer 1978): 385-401.
66. Zashin, "Affirmative Action," pp. 367-368.
67. Rossi, "Sex Equality," p. 184.
68. Gans, *More Equality*, p. 61.
69. Ferber, Loeb, and Lowry, "Economic Status of Women Faculty."
70. Sally Hacker, "Sex Stratification, Technology, and Organizational Change: A Longitudinal Case Study of AT&T," *Social Problems* 26, no. 5 (June 1979): 539-553.
71. Susan Moller Okin, *Women in Western Political Thought* (Princeton, N.J.: Princeton University Press, 1979). Also, Jean Bethke Elshtain, "Antigone's Daughters," *Democracy* (April 1982), pp. 46-59, and "Moral Woman/ Immoral Man: The Public/Private Distinction and Its Political Ramifications," *Politics and Society* 4 (1974).
72. Alan H. Frank, John J. Berman, and Stanley F. Mazur-Hart, "No-Fault Divorce and the Divorce Rate: The Nebraska Experience—An Interrupted Time Series Analysis and Commentary," *Nebraska Law Review* 58, no. 1 (1978): 1-94; Michael Wheeler, *No-Fault Divorce* (Boston: Beacon Press, 1974).
73. Lenore J. Weitzman and Ruth B. Dixon, "The Alimony Myth: Does No-Fault Divorce Make a Difference?" *Family Law Quarterly* 14 (Fall 1980): 141-185.
74. Karen Seal, "A Decade of No-Fault Divorce: What It Has Meant Financially for Women in California," *Family Advocate* 1 (Spring 1979): 10-15.
75. Seal, "A Decade of No-Fault Divorce," p. 14. Emphasis added.
76. Doris Jonas Freed and Henry H. Foster, Jr., "Divorce in the Fifty States: An Overview," *Family Law Quarterly* 14 (Winter 1981): 229-283. Also, Harvey J. Sepler, "Measuring the Effects of No-Fault Divorce Laws across Fifty States: Quantifying a Zeitgeist," *Family Law Quarterly* 15 (Spring 1981): 65-93.
77. Sharon Johnson, "No-Fault Divorce Ten Years Later: Some Virtues, Some Flaws," *New York Times*, March 30, 1979.

5

The Requirements of Political Equality

Political equality between the sexes can only be achieved when gender is irrelevant in evaluating a person's possibilities of functioning successfully in public life. If more political equality is to be realized, feminists must ask for increased participation by women. However, an analysis of their demands shows that, even in asking for greater participation, feminists also ask us to look at the results of the participation. It is not simply participation that counts, but certain kinds of participation with specific kinds of results. Thus feminist positions on voting, office holding, participation in political parties, and interest group activities will be evaluated. The topics intentionally are conventional in order to show that the conventional approach to democratic theory is being profoundly challenged by feminist theory. Indeed, such a challenge is essential for any theory if it proceeds from a perspective that advocates social change rather than maintenance of the status quo.

These four areas of concern are important for increased political equality. If, however, they are not continually evaluated in light of the goals to be achieved, such forms of political participation can simply be used to legitimate existing inequalities. Finally, the importance of the feminist analysis of political participation to the contemporary debate on democratic theory will be discussed.

Voting

Traditionally democratic theorists and feminists have emphasized voting as a significant form of political participation. For voting to be useful in meeting the policy objectives of feminists, four elements must come into play: women must vote and they must do it differently from other groups, women must be able to elect candidates who are feminist—

male and female—and electoral victories must be translated into changes of policy.

Women make up 52.2 percent of all Americans aged eighteen and over. With women living longer than men, the proportion is growing. Furthermore, the gap between the eligible women voters and the eligible male voters has been steadily decreasing. The greater involvement in the social and economic spheres has led to increased voting.[1] In the 1982 election, women turned out in almost the same proportion as men, and they seemed to vote differently enough from men to make a difference in several key elections.[2]

Contemporary feminists do not deny the importance of the vote. It is perhaps the history of the fight for women's suffrage that makes it so clear to feminists, however, that while process is significant, it cannot be the only consideration. Like the poor and the blacks, women have had to struggle for a long time to advance their rights—even longer than the poor men, black or white. Although feminists do not dispute the potential importance of the vote as a means of political participation, they do point to the limits of suffrage in itself as a method of guaranteeing political equality for women. Some fifty years were spent in winning the franchise for women. Recognized as an important achievement, if seen as an end rather than a means, the right to vote is at best meaningless.[3] In other words, the process is important. But the degree of importance can only be measured in terms of policy outcomes.

The women's vote is potentially significant. Women are an increasingly large majority of the electorate. Furthermore, potential power in politics has a force all its own. Elected officials anticipate as many potential voters as possible.[4] Often, strategically located minority groups can take advantage of this potential power. The possibilities for women as a majority of the potential voters are even greater. Thus women involved in feminist causes do have the possibility of referring to their potential support. This advantage can, of course, work in the long run only if certain conditions are met. First of all, women must vote in accordance with their interests as women. As has been demonstrated, that is a very large task in itself. Second, voters must be offered alternatives that will lessen the existing discrimination on the basis of gender. Third, the decisions made by the electorate must be translated into public policy. Voting, by itself, could never lead to a realization of the second and third conditions. Thus, the vote can only be evaluated in the perspective of an analysis of political procedures that includes other forms of political participation as well.

Office Holding

James Bryce writes, "In all assemblies and groups and organized bodies of men, from a nation down to a committee or a club, direction and decision rests in the hands of a small percentage, less and less in proportion to the larger size of the body, till in a great population it becomes an infinitesimally small proportion of the whole number. This is and always has been true of all forms of government, though in different degrees."[5] While it is reasonable to hope that more women will enter public life, certainly the vast majority of the female population will never become public officials. It is crucial to modern democratic theory to examine the degree to which the directions and decisions of government can be concentrated in the hands of the few—that is, women and/or men—and yet that form of government still be called "democratic." The analysis of the concept of "representation" is most significant to any study of political equality.

Very few women are ever elected or appointed to major public office. Indeed, the most striking gender difference in political participation has been the inaccessibility of public office to women. One of the many questions that one must ask is: How represented are women in any executive, legislative, or judicial body which is composed of few or no women? Surely women are not well represented by men or women who are unsympathetic to women's issues, but are women adequately represented even by men who are feminists?[6] How many women, or men sensitive to women's concerns, are necessary in order to guarantee the representation of women?

A representative government requires the machinery to assess the desires of its constituency and that government must respond to those desires unless there are good reasons to the contrary. Contemporary empirically grounded theory has developed several classifications of both the style and focus of representation.[7] Clearly representation cannot require that every citizen have her or his way in every question of public life. It would, of course, be impossible for any officeholder to represent all her or his constituents on every issue—or even on every issue that the constituent is concerned about. Yet if voting is to have any meaning beyond ritual, the elected official must be sensitive to the needs and responsive to the desires of his or her constituency. There need not be a continual activity of responding, but there must be a constant condition of responsiveness or potential readiness to respond. It is not that a government is representative only when it is acting upon an expressed popular wish. A representative government is one which is responsive to popular wishes when there are some. Hence there must be institutional arrangements for responsiveness to these wishes.[8]

There are, of course, many factors that influence the behavior of officeholders. The officeholder is usually a professional politician working within a framework of political institutions, a member of a political party who wants to get re-elected, a member of a judicial or legislative body or administrative officer among peers. She or he must be sensitive to her or his political party, both local and national, and to the various public and private groups and interests. He or she occupies an office to which certain obligations and expectations are attached. Hence, the officeholder must comply with its traditions and work within the framework of the rules and mores. He or she must get along with colleagues, especially certain important ones. To act effectively the officeholder must keep in mind not only the formal and informal rules of his or her office but also its place in the whole structure of government. The complexity of factors involved thus makes questions concerning the nature of representation very difficult to analyze.

The institutional constraints on any one representative are reflected in the literature that has evaluated the differences in the behavior of men and women legislators. One study of local legislators found not much more support for feminist policy among female legislators than among their male counterparts.[9] An analysis of representatives in Congress found few differences in the ways in which men and women perform their congressional role. This was particularly true of those women who were elected on their own and had come up through the same political channel as the men. The study concluded that on most objective measures the women of Congress seem to behave like the men.[10] Surely it should not be surprising to learn that the institution does a great deal to shape the personal behavior of any one of its members, even if the person is a "hippie"-elected mayor, a radical representative, or a woman. Institutions, in turn, are ultimately shaped by some combination of the persons in them and the role the institutions play in the society. We might anticipate that a few women (tokens?)

will adapt to the institutions' expectations. It might well be that representation requires that the governmental institutions have enough women to help shape the expectations of the role. The question then becomes, how many are enough?

In addition to the institutional expectations, individual officeholders will have their own views and opinions on a large variety of issues. They will feel that some measures are intrinsically unsound, immoral, or undesirable, and that some issues are of the highest priority while others might be neglected.[11] At the same time, their opinions may be shaped by those around them and the available sources of information. The representative's opinion on any measure may be influenced by party leaders, by other colleagues, by friends or effective lobbyists, or even by mail. Furthermore, issues do not come before public officials in isolation. Issues are interrelated and the officials may wish to compromise on some in order to gain on others. A particular measure may have some parts to which they respond in varying ways. They may also see measures as having significance beyond their immediate content. For example, the officeholders' gender might play a significant role in shaping what the important issues are to them.

Jo Freeman notes that while several male legislators have sponsored women's legislation, there is usually a woman who is a feminist somewhere in the background. But Freeman also warns that women behind the scenes are not sufficient. It is not enough that women be on congressional staffs, for staff support is hardly adequate to gain congressional support. She emphasizes the importance of having women in Congress who are feminists.[12]

Several studies have found clear differences between the sexes in attitudes toward women's political roles. These include interest in the issues of abortion and the Equal Rights Amendment, interpretation of the Equal Rights Amendment, ratings of various political leaders, willingness to vote for women candidates for political office, and beliefs about the issue orientation of women candidates.[13] Marjorie Randon Hershey explained that sex differences in attitudes toward women candidates are quite dramatic. Women are more favorable to women candidates for each office than men are, and the sex difference increases as the importance and constituency of the office increases. She suggested that the differences on the basis of sex may result from the differential treatment of men and women by the political system. Differential treatment of the two sexes by the political system may produce a sense of biological self-interest. If people believe that they will be treated in politics like all other members of their biological sex, they may conclude that their own situation may improve only as the situation of other members of their biological sex improves.[14]

Kirsten Amundsen urges that feminists must increasingly focus on electing representatives to public office and on seeking top administrative positions for individuals who can be relied on to act in the interests of women. She feels that it is still open to question whether those people can be men as well as women. What is beyond question, however, is that women are likely to gain a more fair and more effective representation if they have more women in decision-making posts. She presumes that there is a politically significant relationship between the proportion of representative positions a group can claim for itself and the degree to which the needs and interests of that group are met.[15]

What about the woman representative who is antifeminist? Or what about the women who are simply not feminists? Certainly there are some political women who have not had their consciousness raised. Like the "welfare Cadillac," this argument inevitably surfaces, probably for similar reasons. It is worthy of attention when a fancy car is seen among poor people or when a women representative takes an antifeminist stand. Meanwhile, poor people waiting for buses or women voting as feminists go unnoticed. A National Women's Political Caucus survey of the women candidates running for election to the state legislatures in 1982 found that 83 percent of the women were supporters of the Equal Rights Amendment and 66 percent were supporters of both the Equal Rights Amendment and prochoice issues.[16]

One study of women in Congress found that they have become, in recent years, a more cohesive group and that the dimensions of their voting behavior are significantly different from their male counterparts. There is a coalition, but if not truly feminist in orientation, it is a feminist coalition. In Congress, gender is not a characteristic that can be ignored.[17] Another study of local women officeholders found that they were more sensitive to charges of discrimination against women and less inclined to view personal commitments at home as insurmountable obstacles to their political careers.[18]

Theories of representation have distinguished between individual and social representation. One study found support for individual women officeholders and particular feminist issues but opposition to the concept of social representation for women.[19] In the 1982 elections much publicity was given to the leading feminist organizations when they supported male candidates in opposition to prominent Congresswomen. Surely there are times when women will not be the best representative of feminist policies. Even more certainly, the liberal ideology supports individual rights and is critical of any group claims. Yet *any* black or *any* woman who is nominated or elected mayor of a major city, appointed to the Supreme Court, or elected president of the United States unavoidably becomes a representative of his or her race or sex.[20] Social representation is unavoidable for women and minorities. In 1960, John F. Kennedy was criticized in several educated Catholic circles because he was not 'Catholic' enough: he did not go to Catholic schools, he would not vote for aid to private schools, and so on. Nonetheless, his election as president erased the liability that all Catholic politicians suffered in their attempts to seek the highest office. Can a similar argument be made about a woman who is not feminist enough? Would a Phyllis Schlafly in the White House and/or the Supreme Court do more for women, in spite of herself, than a male who had profeminist sympathies? Although this is an important question to raise, its answer I believe, is unavoidably unclear. One suspects an antifeminist woman would be preferable to an antifeminist man—and perhaps this will often be the only choice the voter has. The issue emerged recently with the election, indeed the re-election, of Margaret Thatcher as Prime Minister of Great Britain. Certainly, Mrs. Thatcher does not support the kind of public policies that most feminists would favor. Nonetheless, one feminist whose politics are quite different from Mrs. Thatcher's wrote that her election will be most helpful to women. She argues that it will make an enormous difference for all women who want to participate politically because it will help to end the issue of sex as a relevant issue in determining the qualifications of a political candidate.[21] It is difficult to remember now the cultural sanctions against considering a Catholic for president. The electoral success of the "sometimes-ambivalent-about-Catholic-issues" John F. Kennedy totally eliminated Catholicism as a liability for a presidential contender. Gender is undoubtedly a more serious liability than Catholicism. However, any woman being governor, prime minister, or president provides a most dramatic statement that it is possible.

It is also important to question how many young women are able to consider public office after seeing some other (less than perfect) woman fill those roles. Indeed, since women in public office are so rare, the better question to ponder may be how many potentially marvelous women are discouraged from considering public office when they see pictures of the all-male club that politics most often represents. More often than not they learn about politics from male teachers who refer to public officials as "he." After working in the Wisconsin Executive Office for a time and the Wisconsin capitol for several years, this author had the occasion to tour the Connecticut capitol. When the tour guide reached the governor's office, it was pleasantly different to hear her refer to the governor as "she." A less than effective senator, governor, or mayor who is a woman may by her example encourage some talented younger women to persevere in their political aspirations. The presence of women in the job might make it less likely that gender remain the most dominant—and for women the most negative—factor in the eyes of men and women voters.[22] Whenever the issue concerns a disadvantaged group—women or minorities—the issue of appropriate role models is quite significant in the question of representation.[23]

In addition to providing role models to other women, there is evidence that women in public office are more supportive of other women. In departments and agencies headed by women, the record concerning other women's appointments has been far more equitable.[24] Women can and do reinforce their own efforts and those of other women to achieve in the political realm. Women have played a large part in increasing their own presence in representative roles.[25]

While some may argue that, of course, the holding of a policy-making post does not guarantee influence or clout, it is clearly the case that exclusion from such posts virtually ensures lack of influence. "Without a power base, without representatives on the decision-making levels within political institutions," Kirsten Amundsen warns, "citizenship remains but a potential and not an actual resource for groups that are socially and economically disadvantaged." Women must be in legislatures, on top administrative levels, in city councils, on boards of supervisors and on boards of education—in any and all of the institutions where membership presumably opens the way for equal and effective representation.[26] Or, as another feminist put it, "power is elections, and many of our [feminists] will be elected. They will be powerful in terms of being there and making something happen. Their voice will be heard because they pushed that button. And that's where it is at. Pushing the button."[27]

So few women hold public office that it is tempting for feminists to emphasize the need for electing more female officials. When feminists make these demands, they do not argue that more women will automatically entail better representation. They do argue, however, that no women or only a token few women make representation impossible. But feminists also demand more than simply having women in office. They also wish women to act effectively toward reaching certain goals or public policies. Thus the quality of female representation cannot be measured only in numbers of women elected and/or appointed, although certainly greater numbers are needed. Real representation only occurs when women have an effective voice in the decision-making process.

While it is important to get women elected and appointed to public office, election and appointment are not enough.[28] The political power of representatives has to be measured by criteria other than mere holding of office. If a woman is on the White House staff, how much access does she actually have to the president? If a woman is elected to Congress, how important are her committee assignments? Although legislative bodies are composed of equals, some are surely more equal than others. How possible is it for women to become part of the inner circle? How important is it that they do?

Women's roles in public office may be changing. Some of the women recently elected at the national and state levels appear to be developing a different style from that of a passive spectator. One study found that women enjoyed active participation in campaigns and in the political activities of the legislature. They tended to adopt a strategy that made them needed and respected. How this was accomplished is also worth considering. They made themselves respected by becoming subject-matter experts, rather than by becoming one of the "boys."[29] Another study indicated that women candidates and women activists have made great strides in communicating the real meaning of the women's movement to the public. They have projected women's liberation as a movement for equality between the sexes within a framework of basic humanistic goals.[30] Bella Abzug is an example. Feminist supporters regarded Abzug as a candidate who was successful in projecting women's issues onto the national agenda, promoting in Congress and in the nation as a whole issues of concern to women.[31]

To point to Bella Abzug as an effective legislator illustrates a theory developed by Ralph Huitt. He suggested that perhaps the person who becomes "one of the boys" is not the only kind of person who is an effective representative. Huitt argues that it is possible not to be a member of the inner circle nor to feel comfortable in the locker room and still to be an effective legislator. In other words, according to Huitt, there may be at least two kinds of effective role: insider and outsider. Furthermore, the policies the legislator represents may determine the nature of the role chosen. The role that enables a representative to become part of the inner circle might be functional for the groups that benefit from preserving the status quo, yet dysfunctional for those seeking change; functional for the preservation of harmony within the body, yet dysfunctional for conflict resolution in the larger society. The behavior associated with the "outsider" may be functional for protest groups seeking a spokesperson but dysfunctional for groups needing leverage inside the legislative body.[32] Perhaps if they are to have the impact on policy that feminists want them to have, it is inevitable that women legislators be so excluded. It is also possible that exclusion from the inner circles does not inevitably mean lack of effectiveness. Indeed, being an outsider might perhaps be a far more effective role for women who are concerned with the kinds of public policy that feminists advocate.

For example, one of the studies of women in politics claims that by identifying with the oppressed, women in politics have as a group come down heavily on the side of humanism. The authors cite an example:

In Congress Pat Schroeder became an instant thorn in the side of E. Edward Hebert, Louisiana Democrat and Chairman of the House Armed Services Committee, when she obtained a seat over his protest and scandalized the committee by voting for the Cambodia bombing halt. Liz Holtzman initiated a lawsuit that nearly ended the Cambodia bombing. Martha Griffiths led the fight for the Equal Rights Amendment. Edith Green fought for federal aid for higher education. Lenor K. Sullivan led the fight for consumer protection. And Julia Butler Hanse championed a Congressional reform that led to the reorganization of the House of Representatives to give greater power to junior members at the expense of their senior colleagues.[33]

If these women are considered effective legislators, it should be noted that their goals could not have been accomplished even by male members of the inner circle. In concluding his argument for alternative roles in the legislative process, Ralph Huitt argues that the important thing would seem to be not what role is chosen by the legislator, but what the role taker uses it for, and what goals it serves.[34] Thus, again we must look not only at the process but also to where the process leads. The process can only be evaluated in terms of its results.

Political Parties

Certainly the notion of representation is not limited to any one kind of institutional arrangement. Adequate representation can only occur through meaningful participation in public office, political parties, and interest groups. No matter how many women are officeholders, if political equality for women is to become a reality, officeholders who are sympathetic to women's rights must have support from political parties and interest groups. Political parties have often been cited as the institution particularly well suited to ensure the participation of the nonelite in governmental decision making.[35] Parties are an important factor in the concept of representation: they determine the candidates who are offered to the electorate, they provide the organizing principle in the legislative bodies, and they help to structure the public opinion on any given issues.[36] For purposes of political equality it is essential to take into consideration the participation of women in political party activity. This is important because party activity provides a significant opportunity for access to political power, and quite clearly indicates that presence in the corridors of power is not sufficient for actual access to power.

Women traditionally have been very active in political parties. Indeed the vast majority of the work done by political parties is done by women.[37] For the most part, however, their role has been limited to the all too necessary but non-policy-making, non-status-filled positions. They are the foot soldiers of the political parties. Doris Meissner, former executive director of the National Women's Political Caucus, reported on the difficulties of organizing women delegates to the Republican National Convention in 1972. For these women, as Meissner explained, participation alone was not the issue. These women, and women in general, had always been involved in party politics. Meissner explained that "the real question was influence." Although they had been active politically and some even held party offices, they did not have the influence they felt they should have.[38]

Some studies have indicated that there are so few women public officials primarily because the political parties have failed to nominate women for public office.[39] The failure of the parties cannot be attributed to the lack of qualified women candidates. If qualifications are measured in terms of age, occupation, education, training and interest, there are far more qualified women available than have been nominated. Discrimination appears the only factor that can explain the scarcity of women who are nominated by their political parties.[40] Since other studies indicate the voters do not discriminate against female candidates, the main factor that explains why there are so few women public officials seems to be discrimination among party officials. When political parties do nominate women for public office, they nominate them primarily for offices that the women have almost no chances of winning.[41]

Men occupy the positions of power. If the position is merely honorary or symbolic, it is more likely that it will be offered to a woman. Furthermore, since men have a monopoly on the powerful decision-making posts, women can do little to help other women, and most cannot rise in the ranks of the party without the support of a male sponsor. Men generally prefer a certain type of female to sponsor for such a position. They do not want women who are too pushy or too uppity. They want women for whom they feel comfortable opening car doors, helping them on with their coats, and carrying suitcases. They prefer women who are docile, agreeable, supportive, and selfless. Furthermore, they can and do find many such women. In other words, women are selected who will not challenge the male claim to the monopoly of power. It is unlikely that such women will recruit other women in the political system.[42] As within the traditional family, women are quite visible and seldom "equal."

Interest Groups

The major goal of any movement is to politicize or to mobilize its potential members. This is particularly true for a movement that has as potential members over half the population. Feminists are convinced that women are unaware of their present lack of power in the society and even more unaware of the ability to change that situation. The purpose of the women's movement is to transform social conditions—that is, to allow women to see the reality of their present oppression—and to give them the insights and the abilities necessary to change the status quo.

Anyone involved in the antiwar demonstrations of the sixties knows the value of politicizing the potential members of a movement. During that time of mass movements on college campuses, many students, including graduate students in political science, took great pride in their lack of knowledge and/or involvement in the mundaneness of political activities—until they had been clubbed or maced by a state trooper while minding their own business, en route to or studying in the library. After the initial anger and rock-throwing subsided, the knowledge of the potential of the political system for terror remained. Many of those victims became active in the antiwar movement and remain politically active today.[43]

The battle for the passage of the Equal Rights Amendment has been credited with having a similar effect on women.[44] According to Jo Freeman, that struggle involves "politicizing large numbers of women, involving them directly in party and legislative politics, dispelling their self-consciousness and their inhibitions, their feelings of political inadequacy, and their belief in the innate superiority of male politicians. Those women now have a solid, firsthand knowledge of the legislative process and a healthy, hard-won respect for their own ability to change the course of history."[45]

Groups such as the National Organization of Women and the Women's Political Caucus appear to have been instrumental in increasing women's political involvement and heightening their political awareness. One writer in discussing the Women's Political Caucus observed that the traditional party politics apparently did not appeal to a fairly large segment of potentially active middle-class women. She believes that feminist organizations could be able to organize that group. Because of this potential, she predicts that the Women's Political Caucus will have a lasting influence on political participation in the United States.[46] On the other hand, my own experience with the caucus was that it appealed primarily to women who had previously been politically active.[47] The caucus, however, provided the first organization that allowed these women to organize around a political activity that came out of their own personal experience. Women who had previously worked for other candidates and other causes suddenly were able to work for issues of personal concern. Eventually some of them worked for their own candidacy as well. Thus, even if the mobilization is not entirely of different people, the women's movement is organizing women differently from how they have been organized in the past.[48]

Besides motivating more women to participate politically, the movement has encouraged more women to run for office. The number of women being elected to public office at least at the local and state levels has increased dramatically in the last few years.[49] The women's movement has also helped advance women to leadership positions in state legislatures.[50] The authors of a study of the delegates to the 1972 Democratic National Convention also believe that the women's movement was responsible for a change in the kinds of women that became delegates to that convention. In earlier years the typical women representatives to a political convention were widows of important men with large bank accounts. They tended to be selected for their malleability. However, by 1972, a third of the women delegates to the Democratic National Convention were active in the women's movement, and a majority of the women delegates said they had been affected by the movement.[51]

A third important function of interest groups is that they develop policies in the interests of the people they represent. One author writes that "the resurgence of the women's movement in the 1960's focused public awareness on the sexual, social, economic and political inequality in which women found themselves and stimulated scientific research on women within a variety of settings."[52] This author was a delegate to the first Wisconsin Democratic Party State Convention where the issue of abortion was discussed. It was quite uncomfortable to me to listen to the discussion of abortion in an open political forum. I feared that this issue would bring out "crazies" on both sides. I was, of course, by and large right about the level of the political debate that has ensued. Nonetheless, I was ultimately wrong. Although, as I had also anticipated, the most definitive political decision has been made by the United States Supreme Court, it was necessary for the advancement of the rights of women that the issue be raised as a political question. It is the function of the movement to raise these difficult, sometimes embarrassing questions; to make them a legitimate part of the political debate; to get enough support for them that they become law; and to provide the necessary support for their implementation once they do become the law.[53]

Other issues that had seemed to be private that the women's movement has brought into the public debate include rape reform, marital rape, battered women, sexual harassment, and the displaced homemaker. Women's groups have also advocated the elimination of discrimination in pregnancy disability, credit, education, and the military. They have advocated social security reforms, publicly funded day care centers, and flexible work hours. The various women's groups made all of these issues visible.

Another function of interest groups is that they work for the passage of legislation that is in the interest of the groups' constituents. The women's movement is credited with the passage of the Equal Rights Amendment through state legislatures. These groups made their impact through the use of traditional interest-group tactics such as developing their individual abilities to be effective behind the scenes and by performing the research necessary to supply useful information.[54] In Washington, as well, interest groups sympathetic to women's issues used their own communications network to flag the issue during the Equal Rights Amendment struggle and gave it the publicity required for successful lobbying efforts. Some groups put out special flyers, while others included material on the issue in their regular newsletters.[55] According to Jo Freeman, "it is relatively easy to evaluate the effects of the women's liberation movement on the development of women's rights public policy. Prior to the movement there was very little policy on women's status and not much interest in generating more. After the movement had achieved public prominence there was a great deal more."[56]

Since the Congressional passage of the Equal Rights Amendment, various women's groups have organized into a women's lobby. These groups include the League of Women Voters, the National Federation of Business and Professional Women's Clubs, the National Council of Jewish Women, the National Organization of Women, the Women's Equity Action League (WEAL), the Women's Lobby, the National Women's Political Caucus, and various professional business and legally oriented women's groups.[57]

Women's groups have developed more effective use of limited resources by developing specialized interests and dividing areas of specialization. They provide high-level legal research and technical expertise to members of Congress and bureaucrats, which in turn has allowed them to influence the regulation-writing process. Personal lobbying of interested and sympathetic legislators, and constituency pressures placed on those who were less sympathetic, have resulted in many victories.[58] That lobby has been credited with many legislative successes including a minimum wage for domestic workers and laws providing educational equality for women and granting women equal access to credit.[59]

Legislative success, of course, has policy implications. It also has an impact on process. The successful adoption of legislation provides support for further organization.[60] The strength of the group and legislative successes also has an impact on legislative bodies. Members of

Congress have become sensitive to reactions of the potentially active women's groups in their local constituencies. Thus women activists acted as a catalyst, causing legislators to anticipate their constituents' positions. Such anticipations, of course, helped to formulate the constituents' opinions.[61] Furthermore, the existence of a "policy system," which has internalized the values of feminist lobbies and includes within its ranks members of the decision-making system, is supportive of women activists. As a result of this condition crucial information, or feedback, regarding the status of proposed policies has clearly enhanced the position of women activists. For access to decision makers and "monitoring" the status of decisions, a policy network with ongoing contacts is crucial.[62]

It is important to note that the women's movement relied on the assistance of the women members of Congress. Although representatives of women's organizations have reported little face-to-face contact with most members of Congress, the overwhelming exception was in the case of congresswomen. Women members of Congress were the chief sponsors and floor managers of most of the legislation supported by the women's lobby in the first years. The existence of at least a minority of members of Congress who feel intensely enough about a social movement to coordinate and guide its early lobbying seems necessary both for the movement to get a hearing before the legislative body and for it to have a chance for success within that body.[63] Receptivity to feminist issues has been aided by the existence of a caucus of women members of Congress, to which fifteen of the eighteen women representatives belong.[64] The success of the women's groups in changing public policies have been limited, however. Women activists were able to succeed because they played by the "rules of the game." The issue selected was legitimate and noncontroversial. The demands of women activists were specific and challenged no fundamental values of society.[65] They were not successful with issues such as federal funding of day-care centers or abortion.

Having organized support that will reward and punish officeholders for their positions on women's issues is as important as having officeholders who are sympathetic to the public policy concerns of feminists. Thus it becomes quite important for political equality to have an organized, effective women's movement. Organized interest groups representing women's interests are an important factor, if not the most critical, in assuring political equality for women. These groups educate women to their political needs and to the most efficient ways of becoming politically effective in meeting those needs. They also recruit women as political candidates, help them get elected, and give them the support necessary to be effective in their jobs. Likewise, these groups put pressure on all parts of government to pass and implement public policies beneficial to women. They also research, develop, and publicize issues that are to become part of the public policy position of feminist groups.

Feminism and Democratic Theory

A major contribution of feminist literature to contemporary democratic theory is the critique that it provides of the limitations of any theory based on process. Murray Edelman has shown how participation can be manipulated. He argues that "while participation symbolized influence for the powerless, it can also be a key device for their social control."[66] If the rules are written in such a way that participation does nothing but legitimate the procedure—after all the decision-making group did have a student, a faculty person, a minority person, and/or a woman—participation is not only inadequate to meet the requirements for a democratic decision-making procedure, it is counterproductive. Indeed, participation can be manipulated to justify societies and procedures that are antidemocratic.

A study of black participation in urban politics illustrates the problem. The white urban power structure found blacks to appoint and/or to run for public office who were agreeable not to the black community but to the white power structure. Presumably they were supported because they went along with those in power. In other words, they did not represent the black community. The officials voted "white" but could be pointed to as black representatives. The white leadership could have its cake and eat it too.[67]

Surely advocating participation for women involves many dangers. Women in public office may behave no differently from men. It is certainly possible that as representatives of any new group are considered acceptable for membership in any elite political organization, the established members of that institution will try to ensure that only those who meet traditional standards for elite membership are selected. As a result, representatives of the new social group may actually show less deviance from elite norms than members of the dominant elite group.[68]

Furthermore, if the new social group, or women, do not behave the same as the dominant group, or men, they may be ignored or simply given token victories.[69] Undoubtedly, women will be recruited who will work against feminist positions.

There is a potential for those in control of the political institutions to manipulate the processes so as to achieve their ends. The results of such manipulation could have more negative consequences than simply that feminist policies would not be adopted. By concentrating on participation, the women's movement might be effectively eliminated from serious political consideration.[70] Murray Edelman points out that businesses such as ITT influence a great many governmental policies without formal participation, while members of a "therapeutic community" participate all day without significantly changing policy outcomes. As in a therapeutic community, anyone who has ever experienced academic governance of a college or university knows something about the limitations of participation. According to Edelman, those who have the resources can be influential without having to participate formally, and those who lack the resources can use participation only to share in formulating policies that reflect their weaknesses.[71]

I would not carry my critique of the limitations of process quite as far as Edelman does. I am convinced that process can be significant. Clearly women are in a position today where they must make important demands on government. At the same time, they have little influence. Furthermore, if the political processes cannot be made responsive, the future prospects for women are grim indeed. The potential obstacles involved in trying to make the processes responsive are enormous. Nonetheless, the problems are such that there are simply no alternatives except to try. In acting as if there are possibilities, some are created. All of us who are in a position to consider, debate, and write about these problems are too privileged to acquiesce to cynicism. Perhaps in clarifying the goals and identifying the problems, the possible can be made more probable.

How do we know whether participation is democratic participation? The procedures must certainly be evaluated. As with many complex issues, it is much easier to define situations that do not allow for adequate representation than it is to specify the requirements of adequate representation. Political equality for women began to be achieved when women won the right to vote. Voting, however, is only useful if it is possible to vote for candidates who are willing to represent and capable of representing the voters' political interests. Therefore, it *is* important for women to have access to positions of influence and support from political parties and interest groups.

How do we know when we have enough women officeholders so as to ensure adequate representation for women? Hannah Pitkin defines representing as "acting in the interest of the represented, in a manner responsive to them." This definition implies both that the representative exercises his or her own judgment and that he or she listens to the opinions of the constituents. Pitkin goes on to explain: "Political representation is primarily a public, institutional arrangement, involving many people and groups, and operating in the complex ways of large-scale social arrangements. What makes it representation is not any single action by any one participant, but the overall structure and functioning of the system, the patterns emerging from the multiple activities of many people."[72]

Thus representation is a much more complex issue than simply how many women hold public office. The patterns to which Pitkin refers involve public policies that include but are not limited to procedural questions. Feminists argue that it is impossible to represent women in a society that does not have more women officeholders. Process does matter. Women officeholders are a necessary but not a sufficient condition of equal representation. Feminists do not merely demand women officeholders. Rather, they want women representatives who are feminists, and who also have an effective voice in the decision-making process.

Feminists do not need to ask for more female participation in political activities. They must demand more equal participation—and the equality they need is equality of results. Otherwise, women might be in the smoke-filled rooms but ignored—except when it comes time to pour the coffee, empty the ash trays, or chair the ceremonial meetings. They may be allowed to run for office, especially if they are expected to lose.[73] They may even win occasionally or be appointed to an important party or public office, yet they will remain isolated from any real exercise of power. Perhaps they might even be given some power if they do not represent women's interests but are more "loyal" and/or "professional" (that is, male) than the men. Again, it is only when the necessary equality is understood as equality of results that women can become more equal to men in politics.

The most crucial measure of democratic procedure is the quality of public policies that are passed and implemented. When feminists (especially feminists who are not political scientists) discuss political issues, they are primarily concerned with public policy *results*. One feminist argues that the goal is power, which she defines as "teaching women how to increase their input on public policy."[74] Another explains that "it is implementation that determines the ultimate success of any policy sphere. The best indicator of power is policy implementation."[75]

An effective voice does not require winning all of the time, but it does entail winning some of the time. Perhaps feminist issues are more visible to female than to male officeholders. Undoubtedly, women will not receive adequate representation until feminist concerns are given serious consideration in the development of public policy. The best measure of that kind of serious consideration is the kind of policy that is enacted and the manner in which that policy is enforced. In other words, feminists will only consider that there is adequate representation of their interests when some, if not all, of their policy goals are achieved, and all of their demands receive a fair hearing. The number of women necessary in public office equals the number necessary to achieve these public policy goals. The equality that feminists seek is equality of results.

This kind of demand may seem fairly lofty and impossible to achieve, but again Hannah Pitkin's perceptions are worthy of consideration: "The concept of representation thus is a continuing tension between the ideal and achievement. The tension should lead us neither to abandon the ideal, retreating to an operational definition that accepts whatever those usually designed as representatives do, nor to abandon its institutionalization and withdraw from political reality."[76]

Feminism and Contemporary Democratic Theory

Before the twentieth century, democratic theory contained both rules of procedure and certain substantive goals. Based on ideas of the dignity and worth of all persons, it was to be the answer to how people could live together in an organized society with a minimum of coercion. The democrat urged the kind of government in which there was political equality and participation of all citizens. Democracy might never be achieved, but it was, nonetheless, the goal toward which democrats ought to strive.[77]

Since World War II, however, most liberal American writers on democracy have defined it simply in terms of certain procedures.[78] Democracy virtually has become synonymous with electoral politics and civil liberties.

A major debate in contemporary political theory has developed between pluralists and those who argue for participatory democracy.[79] Certainly advocates of participatory democracy do demand more from the process than do the pluralists. They define democracy as a society in which all persons directly involved in a decision have some part in the making of that decision. While the debate between pluralists and advocates of participatory democracy has thrown a great deal of light on many important issues, both theories have a similar limitation: they both concentrate on the governing process rather than on the analysis of public policy or substance. Although the differences between the two groups are very important, the tendency of these schools of thought to stress process rather than policies is a critical point of similarity.

Contemporary definitions of democracy have been criticized by such scholars as Peter Bachrach,[80] Jack Walker,[81] Christian Bay,[82] C. B. Macpherson,[83] and Carole Pateman.[84] The general thrust of their argument is that the process-oriented definitions of democracy lose the value standards involved in the more traditional democratic theories. The critical strength of democratic theory is lost, and a defense and description of the status quo are left in the nations generally considered to be "democratic." An understanding of the problem has been well articulated and has received a great deal of attention. But after understanding the problem, where do we go?

Feminist theory provides the beginning of an answer to that question. The sufficient conditions for a democracy as described by pluralist democrats or by advocates of participatory democracy are inadequate for the kinds of goals feminists wish to achieve. Aware of the efforts involved in achieving women's suffrage, as well as the failure of these efforts to guarantee them political equality, contemporary feminists define political equality as requiring more than an equal vote. Minimally, political equality requires political participation, which includes running for and holding public office. However, all forms of political participation can have the same flaws as the right to vote. Any meaningful claim for political equality between the sexes requires looking beyond process to substance. This does not mean that processes are irrelevant. While changes in procedures are important for achieving certain feminist goals, advocates of equality between the sexes show the limitation inherent in the reliance on any procedures. An analysis of political equality in purely procedural terms is a luxury oppressed people cannot afford. Indeed they will recommend some procedures as being useful in reaching those goals. Procedures are a necessary but not a sufficient condition for political equality.

If the sufficient conditions for political equality could be spelled out in a sentence or a paragraph, then changing the focus of the debate in contemporary democratic theory would be a much easier task. Unfortunately, this cannot be done at "this state of the literature." Nor do I believe that it can ever be done. The issues are too complex and the conditions of public life are continually changing. What can be done, however, is to show the necessity of concentrating on the results of public policies and the need to evaluate the effectiveness of political processes in light of the impact they have on results desired. This is the contribution that feminist theory can make to the development of a contemporary substantive democratic theory.

Most feminists' concerns are not with democratic theory but with improving the living conditions of women. The conditions are bad enough, and efforts to change the conditions encounter such opposition that this concern itself is a very large order. In seeking their goals, however, feminist thought has also implicitly made a valuable contribution to democratic theory. Feminists do not engage in that debate. Rather, they provide an illustration of a substantive argument. Feminist analysis leads to the conclusion that specific results must be seen within a framework that evaluates the effects that particular results will have on all the dimensions of existing inequalities. Feminists argue that public policies must be evaluated to see which policies lead to more and which to less equality between persons. If we do not look at the outcomes, continued and perhaps greater inequalities are guaranteed. No doubt some of the inequalities will be perpetuated in the name of equality.[85]

Political equality is not, of course, the only value that must be discussed in any analysis of democratic theory. Nonetheless equality is a major component of any conception of democracy. Feminists' demands can only be met if equality is understood as equality of results. Furthermore, the results that are demanded require continued evaluation of the public policies adopted if equality is to be achieved. Equality of results does not answer all the questions, but it does direct the analysis to the questions of substance.

In his recent discussion of equality, Robert Dahl argues that procedural democracy is preferable to substantive democracy because it allows for "healthy controversy."[86] It is essential, of course, that any form of democracy allow for differences. In arguing for equality of results, I am neither arguing for absolute equality nor for absolute agreement on the results. I am arguing that all policies must be continually evaluated in terms of the results that they have achieved. This is no claim to a static conception of equality of results. Quite the contrary, it is an argument that recognizes that change occurs continually, that the normal functioning of the system leads to inequality, and that the only way to counteract tendencies toward inequality is to use the norm of equality to evaluate all procedures.

Although he argues against a substantive conception of democracy in favor of procedural democracy, Dahl concedes that procedural democracy does require some substantive goals to be accomplished if the procedures are to function adequately. With this kind of analysis, or with the authors who advocate "substantive" equality of opportunity, it is difficult to know whether there is really an important debate involved in all of this or merely a quibbling over words. Again, the only way to evaluate that problem is to look to the recommendations for change that are made. Dahl lists certain interesting procedural reforms and calls for enlightened understanding on the part of the citizen. However, as with "substantive" demands for equality of opportunity, his recommendations for change are simply not adequate to achieve more equality.[87] Feminist theory clearly shows the inadequacies of such reforms as Dahl suggests. First of all, any procedures, no matter how sophisticated, can be manipulated; and certainly there will always be those who have power and influence and will attempt to do so. Second, the nature of the political must be expanded. There is inevitably a great deal of disagreement about what the sufficient conditions for political equality are. Certainly much of that debate is evident in the feminist literature. Public life is a continually changing phenomenon, and thus I do not expect the conditions required for equality to remain constant. Furthermore, public life is also complex enough that it would be foolish to expect consensus, even among feminists, on the sufficient conditions for equality between the sexes. There is, however, a considerable amount of agreement about the necessary conditions.

Feminists agree that any analysis of political equality must take into consideration economic conditions and socialization factors. Many of its critics have argued that contemporary democratic theory does not take into adequate consideration the significance of economic inequalities in any discussion of political equality.[88] There is also considerable discussion of the problems in a democratic society of citizens not acting in accordance with their own self-interest and/or the public good.[89] Feminist theory gives a clarity of argument and a focus to those issues that can only be seen from the perspective of persons who have been disadvantaged by lack of economic equality and the kind of socialization that inhibits successful functioning in public life. There is now a sizable literature on the comparative position of women and minorities in the United States.[90] Many of the similarities between the problems of women and minorities are accidents of history. There are, of course, also significant differences between the problems of the two groups. One of the crucial similarities is, however, the need for specifying the kind of equality that is required if democratic equality is to provide adequate safeguards for the protection of the rights of women and/or minorities.

Indeed, a valuable perspective on the current controversies surrounding democratic theory can be provided by evaluating those controversies from the view of a disadvantaged group. Admittedly, on the level of theory as well as in practice, this is a stringent test for any theory. But it may well be the difficulty of this test that gives it particular value. Historically, democracy developed as rule by the majority in order to protect the majority from the exploitation of a small, powerful ruling elite. Discussions of democratic theory have involved a great deal of analysis of the strengths and weaknesses of the problems of majority rule. There has also been a considerable analysis of the role of a ruling minority (or minorities). Eventually political theorists and others realized that majority rule could also be majority tyranny and they expressed concern that the rights of the minorities must be written into any procedures. Thus much of the writing in political theory has involved the rights of the majority balanced against the rights of the minorities. Indeed, this balancing is a very difficult problem for democratic theory.

An even more difficult challenge for democratic theory, however, is the challenge of developing the theory to the point of recognizing the likelihood that certain groups have been discriminated against in any society, and that in all societies such discrimination is written into the institutions of the society. Feminists make this point very clear. They have done an excellent job in reformulating the questions that should be asked. They show that political equality requires some control over economic conditions, including adequate salaries and meaningful jobs;

nonoppressive personal relationships that stress the worth and dignity of each individual; and public policy that takes into account the needs and wants of all the citizens. The kind of democratic theory that would mandate a meaningful equality between the sexes might well be used to protect unpopular minorities from exploitation and unnecessary coercion—even when the discrimination is less obvious and/or more subtle than in the case of discrimination on the basis of gender or race. Any attempt to counteract all such discrimination, short of a revolution, must be directed at changing the institutional arrangements that perpetuate the discrimination. Process is important. Nonetheless, if change is to lead to more equality, the main emphasis must be on the goals to be achieved. Furthermore, it should also be anticipated that attempts at changing the status quo will only be marginally successful. Such margins, of course, can be most significant to the persons involved.

Notes

1. Marjorie Lansing and Sandra Baxter, *Women and Politics: The Invisible Majority* (Ann Arbor: University of Michigan Press, 1981).
2. Gloria Steinem, "Post-ERA Politics: Losing a Battle but Winning the War?" *Ms.*, January 1983, p. 66.
3. Kirsten Amundsen, *A New Look at the Silenced Majority: Women and American Democracy* (Englewood Cliffs, N.J.: Prentice-Hall, 1977), p. 61; Jo Freeman, *The Politics of Women's Liberation* (New York: David McKay Co., 1975); Shulamith Firestone, *The Dialectic of Sex: The Case for Feminist Revolution* (New York: Bantam Books, 1970), pp. 21-22; Juliet Mitchell, *Women's Estate* (New York: Vintage Books, 1970), pp. 35-36.
4. Robert A. Dahl, *Who Governs? Democracy and Power in an American City* (New Haven, Conn.: Yale University Press, 1961).
5. James Bryce, *Modern Democracies* (New York: Macmillan Co., 1924), p. 542.
6. Jo Freeman, *Politics*, pp. 204-205.
7. Heinz Eulau, John C. Whalke, William Buchanan, and LeRoy C. Ferguson, "The Role of the Representative: Some Empirical Observations on the Theory of Edmund Burke," *American Political Science Review* (September 1959): 742-56; John C. Whalke and Heinz Eulau, *The Legislative System* (New York: John Wiley & Sons, 1962).
8. Hannah Fenichel Pitkin, *The Concept of Representation* (Berkeley: University of California Press, 1967), pp. 232-233.

9. Susan Gluck Mezey, "Support for Women's Rights Policies: An Analysis of Local Politicians," *American Politics Quarterly* 6 (October 1978): 497.

10. Frieda L. Gehlen, "Women Members of Congress: A Distinctive Role," in *A Portrait of Marginality: The Political Behavior of the American Woman*, ed. Marianne Githens and Jewel L. Prestage (New York: David McKay Co., 1977), pp. 317-18.

11. Charles S. Bullock, III, and Patricia Lee Findley Heys, "Recruitment of Women for Congress: A Research Note," *Western Political Quarterly* 25 (September 1972): 416-23; Kathleen A. Frankovic, "Sex and Voting in the U.S. House of Representatives, 1961-1975," *American Politics Quarterly* 5 (July 1977): 315-330.

12. Jo Freeman, *Politics*, pp. 204-205.

13. Marjorie Randon Hershey, "The Politics of Androgyny? Sex Roles and Attitudes toward Women in Politics," *American Politics Quarterly* 5 (July 1977): 271-274; Laurie E. Ekstrand and William A. Eckert, "The Impact of Candidates' Sex on Voter Choice," *Western Political Quarterly* 35 (March 1981): 85.

14. Hershey, "Politics of Androgyny?" pp 284-285.

15. Amundsen, *Silenced Majority*, p. 62.

16. Steinem, "Post-ERA Politics," p. 66.

17. Frankovic, "Sex and Voting," p. 329.

18. Mezey, "Support for Women's Rights," p. 494.

19. Jerry Perkins and Diane L. Fowlkes, "Opinion Representation versus Social Representation; or, Why Women Can't Run as Women and Win," *American Political Science Review* 74, no. 1 (March 1980): 92-103.

20. Virginia Sapiro, "When Are Interests Interesting?" *American Political Science Review* 75, no. 3 (September 1981): 711.

21. Susan Sontag, "On the Meaning of Margaret Thatcher," *Ms.*, July 1979, p. 68.

22. Women face this prejudice from members of both sexes. A 1970 Gallup Poll found that 13 percent of both men and women would not vote for a woman candidate for Congress—even if they considered her to be qualified. The number is even higher when it is the presidency that is at issue. See Naomi Lynn, "Women in American Politics: An Overview," in Jo Freeman, *Women: A Feminist Perspective* (Palo Alto, Calif.: Mayfield, 1975), p. 372. Also see Sarah Slavin Schramm, "Women and Representation: Self-Government and Role Change," *Western Political Quarterly* 34 (March 1981): 58.

23. For an excellent analysis and review of the literature on women's political participation, see Bonnie Cook Freeman, "Power, Patriarchy, and 'Political Primitives,' " in *Beyond Intellectual Sexism: A New Woman, New Reality*, ed. Joan I. Roberts (New York: David McKay Co., 1976), pp. 241-264. See particularly p. 253.

24. Susan Carroll, "Recruitment during a Period of Elite Circulation: The Case of Women Appointed to the Carter Administration." Paper presented at the 1982 Annual Meeting of the Midwest Political Science Association, Milwaukee, Wis., April 28-May 1.

25. Schramm, "Women and Representation," p. 59. Also, Ellen Boneparth, "Women in Campaigns: From Lickin' and Stickin' to Strategy," *American Politics Quarterly* 5 (July 1977): 293-294.

26. Amundsen, *Silenced Majority*, pp. 61-62.

27. Susan and Martin Tolchin, *Clout: Womanpower and Politics* (New York: Capricorn Books, 1973), p. 204.

28. Amundsen, *Silenced Majority*, p. 66.

29. Bonnie Cook Freeman, "Power, Patriarchy, and 'Political Primitives,'" p. 256.

30. Tolchin, *Clout*, p. 227.

31. Tolchin, *Clout*, p. 171.

32. Ralph K. Huitt, "The Outsider in the Senate: An Alternative Role," *American Political Science Review* 55, no. 3 (September 1961). See also Irene Diamond, *Sex Roles in the State House* (New Haven, Conn.: Yale University Press, 1977), p. 170.

33. Tolchin, *Clout*, p. 246.

34. Huitt, "Outsider in the Senate," p. 573.

35. See James MacGregor Burns, *The Deadlock of Democracy* (Englewood Cliffs, N.J.: Prentice-Hall, 1964). There are those who argue that political parties actually inhibit political participation. C. B. Macpherson, *The Life and Times of Liberal Democracy* (London: Oxford University Press, 1977), pp. 64-67. While that might well be the case today, I do not believe that this inhibition is intrinsic to the party system. Indeed, if the kinds of representation that are demanded in this section were realized, I believe that much of the criticism of the role of parties would be met.

36. Maurice Duverger, *Political Parties* (New York: John Wiley & Sons, 1959), p. 381.

37. Harold D. Clarke and Allan Kornberg, "Moving Up the Political Escalator: Women Party Officials in the United States and Canada," *Journal of Politics* 41, no. 2 (May 1979): 442-477; Susan Welch, "Women as Political Animals? A Test of Some Explanations for Male-Female Political Participation Differences," *American Journal of Political Science* 21, no. 4 (November 1977): 721.

38. Tolchin, *Clout*, p. 232.

39. Diane Fowlkes, Jerry Perkins, Sue Tolleson Rinehart, "Gender Roles and Party Roles," *American Political Science Review* 73 (September 1979): 772-780; R. Darcy and Sarah Slavin Schramm, "When Women Run against Men," *Public Opinion Quarterly* 41 (Spring 1977): 1-12.

40. Wilma Rule, "Why Women Don't Run: The Critical Contextual Factors in Women's Legislative Recruitment," *Western Political Quarterly* 34 (March 1981): 76-77.

41. Nikki R. Van Hightower, "The Recruitment of Women for Public Office," *American Politics Quarterly* 5 (July 1977): 312.

42. Bonnie Cook Freeman, "Power, Patriarchy, and 'Political Primitives,' " p. 253.

43. Political activity does not of course guarantee success. Perhaps the major result of political activity in 1968 was the defeat of Hubert Humphrey and the election of Richard Nixon; also see Sara Evans, *Personal Politics* (New York: Vintage Books, 1979).

44. Tolchin, *Clout*, p. 115. Also please note that Jo Freeman does distinguish social movements from interest group activities (*Politics*, p. 46); for purposes of this analysis, however, I will ignore the distinctions that she makes. Anne N. Costain, "Representing Women: The Transition from Social Movement to Interest Group," *Western Political Quarterly* 33 (June 1980): 106; Joyce Gelb and Marian Lief Palley, "Women and Interest Group Politics: A Case Study of the Equal Credit Opportunity Act," *American Politics Quarterly* 5 (July 1977): 335.

45. Jo Freeman, *Politics*, p. 67.

46. Barbara Burrell, "A New Dimension in Political Participation: The Women's Political Caucus," in Githens and Prestage, *A Portrait of Marginality*. p. 242.

47. I was on the Wisconsin State Board of the Wisconsin Political Caucus in 1972.

48. Firestone's *Feminist Revolution* makes a similar argument. See particularly pp. 92-96.

49. Virginia Currey, "Campaign Theory and Practice: The Gender Variable," in Githens and Prestage, *A Portrait of Marginality*, p. 151; Steinem, "Post-ERA."

50. Tolchin, *Clout*, p. 115.

51. John W. Soule and Wilma E. McGrath, "A Comparative Study of Male and Female Political Attitudes at Citizen and Elite Levels," in Githens and Prestage, *A Portrait of Marginality*, p. 151.

52. Githens and Prestage, *A Portrait of Marginality*, p. 4.

53. Gelb and Palley, "Women and Interest Group Politics: A Case Study," p. 337.

54. Tolchin, *Clout*, pp. 115-116.

55. Tolchin, *Clout*, p. 139.

56. Jo Freeman, *Politics*, pp. 233-234.

57. Joyce Gelb and Marian Lief Palley, "Women and Interest Group Politics: A Comparative Analysis of Federal Decision-Making," *Journal of Politics* 41, no. 2 (May 1979): 364.

58. Gelb and Palley, "Women and Interest Group Politics: A Case Study," p. 335.
59. Costain, "Representing Women," p. 110; Gelb and Palley, "Women and Interest Group Politics: A Case Study," p. 335.
60. Anne N. Costain, "The Struggle for a National Women's Lobby: Organizing a Diffuse Interest," *Western Political Science Quarterly* 4 (December 1980): 484.
61. Gelb and Palley, "Women and Interest Group Politics: A Comparative Analysis," p. 368.
62. Gelb and Palley, "Women and Interest Group Politics: A Comparative Analysis," p. 389.
63. Costain, "Representing Women," pp. 111-112.
64. Gelb and Palley, "Women and Interest Group Politics: A Comparative Analysis," p. 389; and their "Women and Interest Group Politics: A Case Study," p. 346.
65. Gelb and Palley, "Women and Interest Group Politics: A Case Study," p. 350.
66. Murray Edelman, "The Language of Participation and the Language of Resistance," *Human Communication* 3, no. 2 (Winter 1977): 159.
67. Karl H. Flaming, J. John Palen, Grant Ringlien and Corneff Taylor, "Black Powerlessness in Policy-Making Positions," in *City Scenes*, ed. J. John Palen (Boston: Little, Brown & Co., 1977).
68. Kenneth Prewitt and Alan Stone, *The Ruling Elite* (New York: Harper & Row, 1973); Carroll, "Recruitment," p. 18; Diamond, *Sex Roles*; Mezey, "Support for Women's Rights," p. 496.
69. Van Hightower, "Recruitment of Women," p. 312.
70. Sapiro, "When Are Interests Interesting?" p. 710.
71. Edelman, "Language," p. 160.
72. Pitkin, *The Concept of Representation*, pp. 221-22.
73. See Elizabeth G. King, "Women in Iowa Legislative Politics," in Githens and Prestage, *Portrait of Marginality*, p. 291. This point is also made by Cook Freeman and Lynn.
74. Tolchin, *Clout*, p. 231
75. Jo Freeman, *Politics*, p. 11.
76. Pitkin, *Concept of Representation*, p. 256.
77. For further elaboration of this argument see Graeme Duncan and Steven Lukes, "Democracy Restated," and Lane Davis, "The Cost of the New Realism," both in *Frontiers of Democratic Theory*, ed. Henry S. Kariel (New York: Random House, 1970).
78. Henry Mayo offers a good example of this view of democracy. His working definition of democracy is that the "democratic political system is one in which public policies are made on a majority basis by representatives subject

to effective popular control at periodic elections, which are conducted on the principle of political equality under conditions of political freedom." Henry B. Mayo, *An Introduction to Democratic Theory* (New York: Oxford University Press, 1960), p. 70.

79. Robert Booth Fowler and Jeffery R. Orenstein, *Contemporary Issues in Political Theory* (New York: John Wiley & Sons, Inc., 1977), pp. 3, 43.

80. Peter Bachrach, *The Theory of Democratic Elitism: A Critique* (Boston: Little, Brown & Co., 1967); and his *Political Elites in a Democracy* (New York: Atherton Press, 1971).

81. Jack B. Walker, "Normative Consequences of Democratic Theory," in Kariel, *Frontiers of Democratic Theory*.

82. Christian Bay, *The Structure of Freedom* (Stanford, Calif.: Stanford University Press, 1970); and his "Civil Disobedience: Prerequisite for Democracy in Mass Society," in *Obligation and Dissent: An Introduction to Politics*, ed. Donald W. Hanson and Robert Booth Fowler (Boston: Little, Brown & Co., 1971).

83. C. B. Macpherson, *The Real World of Democracy* (London: Oxford University Press, 1971); and his *Democratic Theory: Essays in Retrieval* (London: Oxford University Press, 1973), and *The Life and Times of Liberal Democracy* (London: Oxford University Press, 1977).

84. Carole Pateman, *Participation and Democratic Theory* (Cambridge: Cambridge University Press, 1970).

85. Jean Bethke Elshtain, "The Feminist Movement and the Question of Equality," *Polity* 7, no. 4 (Summer 1975): 471.

86. Robert A. Dahl, "On Removing Certain Impediments to Democracy in the United States," *Dissent* 25 (Summer 1978): 319.

87. Dahl, "Impediments," p. 322.

88. Macpherson, *Democratic Theory*, especially p. 170. Dahl also discusses the economic preconditions for democracy in his "Impediments" article in *Dissent*. He does not, however, include that argument in his recommendations for reforms. Also see Philip Green and Robert A. Dahl, "What Is Political Equality?" *Dissent* 25 (Summer 1979): 351-368.

89. Isaac D. Balbus, "The Concept of Interest in Pluralist and Marxian Analysis," *Politics and Society* 2 (February 1971): 151-177; also Charlotte G. O'Kelly, "The 'Impact' of Equal Employment Legislation on Women's Earnings: Limitations of Legislative Solutions to Discrimination in the Economy," *American Journal of Sociology* 38, no. 4 (October 1979): 419-429.

90. M. V. Belok, "Women: A Forgotten Minority," *Journal of Thought* (November 1969): 273-277, and "Sexism and Racism Symposium," *Civil Rights Digest* 5-6 (Spring 1974): 2-81; Helen Hacker Mayer, "Women as a Minority Group," in *Women: A Feminist Perspective*, ed. Jo Freeman (Palo Alto, Calif.: Mayfield, 1975), pp. 402-415; Joreen, "The 51 Percent Minority

Group: A Statistical Essay," in *Sisterhood Is Powerful*, ed. Robin Morgan (New York: Vintage Books, 1970), pp. 455-468; Faith A. Seidenberg, "The Submissive Majority: Modern Trends in the Law concerning Women's Rights," *Cornell Law Review* 55 (1969-70); Joyce Trebilcot, "Sex Roles: The Argument from Nature," *Ethics* 85 (April 1975): 249-255.

Bibliography

Abzug, Bella. "Forming a Real Women's Bloc." *The Nation*, November 28, 1981, pp. 576-578.

Acker, Joan. "Women and Social Stratification: A Case of Intellectual Sexism." In *Changing Woman in a Changing Society*, edited by Joan Huber, pp. 174-183. Chicago: University of Chicago Press, 1973.

Ahart, Gregory J. "A Process Evaluation of the Contract Compliance Program in Nonconstruction Industry." *Industrial and Labor Relations Review* 29 (July 1976): 565-584.

Amundsen, Kirsten. *A New Look at the Silenced Majority: Women and American Democracy*. Englewood Cliffs, N.J.: Prentice-Hall, 1977.

Ayella, Mary Elizabeth, and Williamson, John B. "The Social Mobility of Women: A Causal Model of Socioeconomic Success." *Sociological Quarterly* 17 (Autumn 1976): 534-554.

Bachrach, Deborah. "Women in Employment." *Clearinghouse Review/National Clearinghouse for Legal Services* 14 (February 1981): 1041-1047.

Bachrach, Deborah, et al. "Women and Poverty: Women's Issues in Legal Services Practice." *Clearinghouse Review/National Clearinghouse for Legal Services* 14 (February 1981): 1035-1041.

Bachrach, Peter. *Political Elites in a Democracy*. New York: Atherton Press, 1971.

——. *The Theory of Democratic Elitism: A Critique*. Boston: Little, Brown & Co., 1967.

Baer, Denise L. "Biology, Gender, and Politics: An Assessment and Critique." Presented at the Annual Meeting of the Midwest Political Science Association. Milwaukee, Wis., April 29-May 1, 1982.

Balbus, Isaac D. "The Concept of Interest in Pluralist and Marxian Analysis." *Politics and Society* 2 (February, 1971): 151-177.

Barogun, Barbara. "Marriage as an Oppressive Institution/Collectives as Solutions." In *Voices from Women's Liberation*, edited by Leslie B. Tanner, pp. 296-302. New York: New American Library, 1970.

Barry, Brian. *Political Argument*. New York: Humanities Press, 1965.

Baumer, Donald C.; Van Horn, Carl E.; and Marvel, Mary. "Explaining Benefit Distribution in CETA Programs." *Journal of Human Resources* 14, no 2.

Baxandall, Rosalyn R. "Who Shall Care for Our Children? The History of Development of Day Care in the United States." In *Women: A Feminist Perspective*, edited by Jo Freeman, pp. 88-102. Palo Alto, Calif.: Mayfield, 1975.

Baxter, Sandra, and Lansing, Marjorie. *Women and Politics: The Invisible Majority.* Ann Arbor: University of Michigan Press, 1981.

Bay, Christian. "Behavioral Research and the Theory of Democracy." In *Frontiers of Democratic Theory*, edited by Henry S. Kariel, pp. 164-188. New York: Random House, 1970.

———. "Civil Disobedience: Prerequisite for Democracy in Mass Society." In *Obligation and Dissent: An Introduction to Politics*, edited by Donald W. Hanson and Robert Booth Fowler, pp. 222-242. Boston: Little, Brown & Co., 1971.

———. *The Structure of Freedom.* Stanford, Calif.: Stanford University Press, 1970.

Beatty, Kathleen M., and Walter, B. Oliver. "Sex Related Issue Attitudes: The Effects of Religion and Situation." Presented at the Annual Meeting of the Midwest Political Science Association. Cincinnati, Ohio, April 16-18, 1981.

Beck, E. M.; Horan, Patrick M.; and Tolbert, Charles M. "Stratification in a Dual Economy: A Sectoral Model of Earnings Determination." *American Sociological Review* 43 (October 1978): 704-720.

Beckwith, Karen. "The Public-Private Distinction and Why Women Can't Be Citizens." Presented at the Annual Meeting of the Midwest Political Science Association. Cincinnati, Ohio, April 16-18, 1981.

Bedau, Hugo Adam. "Egalitarianism and the Idea of Equality." In *Nomos IX: Equality.* Edited by J. Roland Pennock and John W. Chapman, pp. 3-27. New York: Atherton Press, 1967.

Belok, M. V. "Sexism and Racism Symposium." *Civil Rights Digest* 5-6 (Spring 1974): 2-18.

———. "Women: A Forgotten Minority." *Journal of Thought* (November, 1969): 273-277.

Benn, S. I., "Egalitarianism and the Equal Consideration of Interest." In *Nomos: IX Equality*, edited by J. Roland Pennock and John W. Chapman, pp. 51-78. New York: Atherton Press, 1967.

Benn, S. I., and Peters, R. S. *The Principles of Political Thought.* New York: Free Press, 1959.

Benston, Margaret. "The Political Economy of Women's Liberation." *Monthly Review* (September 1969).

Berlin, Sir Isaiah. "Equality as an Ideal." In *Justice and Social Policy*, edited by Frederick A. Olafson, pp. 120-135. Englewood Cliffs, N.J.: Prentice-Hall, 1961.

Bernard, Shirley. "Women's Economic Status: Some Clichés and Some Facts." In *Women: A Feminist Perspective*, edited by Jo Freeman, pp. 238-242. Palo Alto, Calif.: Mayfield, 1975.

Bessmer, Sue. "Anti-Obscenity: A Comparison of the Legal and the Feminist Perspectives." *Western Political Quarterly* 34 (March 1981): 143-155.

Blackstone, William T. "Freedom and Women." *Ethics* (April 1975): 243-248.

Blau, Francine D., and Hendricks, Wallace E. "Occupational Segregation by Sex: Trends and Prospects." *Journal of Human Resources* 14 (Spring 1979): 197-210.

Blau, Peter M., and Duncan, Otis D. *The American Occupational Structure*. New York: John Wiley & Sons, 1967.

Blauner, Robert. "Whitewash over Watts." *Transaction* 3 (March-April 1966).

Bluestone, Barry; Murphy, William H.; and Stevenson, Mary H. *Low Wages and the Working Poor*. The Institute of Labor and Industrial Relations. Ann Arbor: University of Michigan, Wayne State University, 1973.

Blumrosen, Ruth G. "Wage Discrimination and Job Segregation: The Survival of a Theory." *University of Michigan Journal of Law Reform* 14 (Fall 1980): 1-14.

———. "Wage Discrimination, Job Segregation, and Title VII of the Civil Rights Act of 1964." *University of Michigan Journal of Law Reform* 12 (Spring 1979): 399-503.

Boles, Janet K. "The Equal Rights Amendment as a Non-Zero-Sum Game." Presented at the Hutchins Center for the Study of Democratic Institutions, October 27, 1981.

Bonacich, Edna. "Advanced Capitalism and Black/White Race Relations in the United States: A Split Labor Market Interpretation." *American Sociological Review* 41 (February 1976): 34-51.

Boneparth, Ellen. "Women in Campaigns: From Lickin' and Stickin' to Strategy." *American Politics Quarterly* 5 (July 1977): 289-300.

Boundy, Kathleen B. "Sex Inequities in Education." *Clearinghouse Review/ National Clearinghouse for Legal Services* 14 (February 1981): 1048-1056.

Bourque, Susan D., and Grossholtz, Jean. "Politics, an Unnatural Practice: Political Science Looks at Female Participation." *Politics and Society* 4 (Winter 1974): 258.

Bowman, Ann. "Physical Attractiveness and Electability: Looks and Votes." Presented at the Annual Meeting of the Midwest Political Science Association. Chicago, Ill. April 24-26, 1980.

Boxill, Bernard R. "Sexual Blindness and Sexual Equality." *Social Theory and Practice* 6 (Fall 1980): 281-298.

Brandt, Richard. *Social Justice*. Englewood Cliffs, N.J.: Prentice-Hall, 1962.

Brennan, Teresa, and Pateman, Carole. "Mere Auxiliaries to the Commonwealth: Women and the Origins of Liberalism." *Political Studies* 27 (June 1979): 183-200.

Brown, Gary D. "Discrimination and Pay Disparities between White Men and Women." *Monthly Labor Review* 101 (March 1978): 17-22.

Bryce, James. *Modern Democracies*. New York: Macmillan Co. 1924.

Bullock, Charles S., III, and Heys, Patricia Lee Findley. "Recruitment of Women for Congress: A Research Note." *Western Political Quarterly* 25 (September 1972): 416-423.

Burns, James MacGregor. *The Deadlock of Democracy*. Englewood Cliffs, N.J.: Prentice-Hall, 1964.

Burrell, Barbara. "A New Dimension in Political Participation: The Women's Political Caucus." In *A Portrait of Marginality: The Political Behavior of the American Woman* edited by Marianne Githens and Jewel L. Prestage, pp. 241-263. New York: David McKay Co., Inc., 1977.

California Commission on the Status of Women. *Impact ERA: Limitations and Possibilities*. Millbrae, Calif.: Les Femmes Publishing, 1976.

Caplan, Nathan S., and Paige, Jeffery. "A Study of Ghetto Rioters." *Scientific American* 219 (August 1968).

Carmichael, Stokely, and Hamilton, Charles V. *Black Power*. New York: Vintage Books, 1967.

Carroll, Susan. "Recruitment during a Period of Elite Circulation: The Case of Women Appointed to the Carter Administration." Presented at the Annual Meeting of the Midwest Political Science Association. Milwaukee, Wis., April 29-May 1, 1982.

Carter, Barbara L., and Newman, Dorothy K. "Perceptions about Black Americans." *Annals of the American Academy of Political and Social Science* (January 1978): 17-20.

Castelnuovo, Shirley. "The Liberal Legal Paradigm and Its Impact on the Judicial Process Regarding Preferential Treatment." Presented at the American Political Science Association Meeting. Washington, D.C., August 30-September 2, 1979.

Catlin, George E. G., "Equality and What We Mean by It." In *Nomos IX: Equality*, ed. J. Roland Pennock and John W. Chapman, pp. 99-111. New York: Atherton Press, 1967.

Cavanagh, Thomas E. "The Calculus of Representation: A Congressional Perspective." *Western Political Quarterly* 35 (March 1982): 120-129.

Celarier, Michelle. "Money: The Paycheck Challenge of the Eighties—Comparing Job Worth." *Ms.*, March 1981.

Chenoweth, Lillian, and Maret-Havens, Elizabeth. "Women's Labor Force Participation: A Look at Some Residential Patterns." *Monthly Labor Review* 101 (March 1978): 38-41.

Chodorow, Nancy. *The Reproduction of Mothering: Psychoanalysis and the Sociology of Gender.* Berkeley: University of California Press, 1978.

Christy, Carol A. "Cross-National Patterns in Sex Differences in Political Participation." Presented at the Annual Meeting of the Midwest Political Science Association. Cincinnati, Ohio, April 16-18, 1981.

Church, George J. "Every Man for Himself." *Time*, September 7, 1981, pp. 8-9.

Clarke, Harold D., and Kornberg, Allan. "Moving up the Political Escalator: Women Party Officials in the United States and Canada." *Journal of Politics* 41, no. 2 (May 1979): 442-477.

Cohen, Marshall; Nagel, Thomas; and Scanlon, Thomas, eds. *Equality and Preferential Treatment.* Princeton, N.J.: Princeton University Press, 1977.

Cohler, Anne. "Women in the Spirit of the Times." Presented at the Annual Meeting of the Midwest Political Science Association. Milwaukee, Wis., April 29-May 1, 1982.

Conlin, Roxanne Barton. "The Legal Status of Homemakers in Michigan." Homemakers Committee, National Commission on the Observance of International Women's Year. June 1977.

Constantini, Edmund, and Craik, Kenneth H. "Women as Politicians: The Social Background, Personality, and Political Careers of Female Party Leaders." *Journal of Social Issues* 28 (1972).

Constantini, Edmund; Craik, Kenneth H.; and Mezey, Susan Gluck. "Does Sex Make a Difference? A Case Study of Women in Politics." *Western Political Quarterly* 31 (1978): 492-501.

Cook, Beverly Blair. "Sex Roles and the Burger Court." *American Politics Quarterly* 5 (July 1977).

Cook, Karen S., and Emerson, Richard M. "Power, Equity, and Commitment in Exchange Networks." *American Sociological Review*, 43 (October 1978).

Cooper, W. E. "What Is Sexual Equality and Why Does Tey Want It?" *Ethics*, April 1975.

Corcoran, Mary, and Duncan, Greg J. "Work History, Labor Force Attachment, and Earnings Differences between the Races and Sexes." *Journal of Human Resources* 14 (Winter 1979).

Cord, Steven B. "Equal Rights: A Provable Moral Standard." *American Journal of Economics and Sociology* 38 (January 1979).

Coser, Rose Lamb, and Rokoff, Gerald. "Women in the Occupational World: Social Disruption and Conflict." *Social Problems* 18 (September 1971).

Costain, Anne N. "Representing Women: The Transition from Social Movement to Interest Group." *Western Political Quarterly* 33 (June 1980): 100-113.

———. "The Struggle for a National Women's Lobby: Organizing a Diffuse Interest." *Western Political Science Quarterly* 4 (December 1980): 476-491.

Crowell, Suzanne. "Four Days in Houston: Watershed for Women's Rights?" *Civil Rights Digest* 10 (Winter 1978): 3-13.

Currey, Virginia. "Campaign Theory and Practice: The Gender Variable." In *A Portrait of Marginality: Political Behavior of the American Woman*, edited by Marianne Githens and Jewel L. Prestage, pp. 165-172. New York: David McKay Co., 1977.

Dahl, Robert A. "On Removing Certain Impediments to Democracy in the United States." *Dissent* 25 (Summer 1978): 310-324.

———. *Who Governs? Democracy and Power in an American City*. New Haven, Conn.: Yale University Press, 1961.

Darcy, R., and Schramm, Sarah Slavin. "When Women Run against Men." *Public Opinion Quarterly* 41 (Spring 1977): 1-12.

Davis, Joe C., and Hubbard, Carl M. "On the Measurement of Discrimination against Women." *American Journal of Economics and Sociology* 38 (July 1979): 287-291.

Davis, Kingsley, and Moore, Wilbert E. "Some Principles of Stratification." *American Sociological Review* 10 (April 1945).

Deaux, Kay, and Emswiller, Tim. "Explanation of Successful Performance in Sex Linked Tasks: What Is Skill for the Male Is Luck for the Female." *Journal of Personality and Social Psychology* 29, no. 1 (1974): 80-85.

Deber, Raisa B. "The Fault, Dear Brutus: Women as Congressional Candidates in Pennsylvania." Presented at the Annual Meeting of the Midwest Political Science Association. Chicago, Ill., April 24-26, 1980.

Deckard, Barbara, and Sherman, Howard. "Monopoly Power and Sex Discrimination." *Politics and Society* 4, no. 4 (1974): 480-481.

Deckard, Barbara Sinclair. *The Women's Movement: Political, Socioeconomic and Psychological Issues*. New York: Harper and Row, 1975.

Diamond, Irene. *Sex Roles in the State House*. New Haven, Conn.: Yale University Press, 1977.

Diamond, Irene, and Hartsock, Nancy. "Beyond Interest in Politics: A Comment on Virginia Sapiro's 'When Are Interests Interesting?' The Problem of Political Representation of Women." *American Political Science Review* 75, no. 3 (September 1981): 717-721.

Dinnerstein, Dorothy. *The Mermaid and the Minotaur*. New York: Harper Colophon Books, 1977.

Downs, Elizabeth. "Evaluation of Michigan's Pilot Displaced Homemakers Project." Michigan Department of Labor, June 1981.

Dubeck, Paula J. "Women and Access to Political Offices: A Comparison of Female and Male State Legislators." *Sociological Quarterly* 17 (Winter 1976): 42-52.

Duncan, R. Paul, and Perrucci, Carolyn Cummings. "Dual Occupation Families and Migration." *American Sociological Review* 41 (April 1976): 252-261.

Duverger, Maurice. *Political Parties*. New York: John Wiley & Sons, 1959.

Edelman, Murray. "The Language of Participation and the Language of Resistance." *Human Communication* 3, no. 2 (Winter 1977): 156-163.

———. *The Symbolic Uses of Politics*. Urbana, Ill.: University of Illinois Press, 1964.

Eder, Donna, and Hallinan, Maureen T. "Sex Differences in Children's Friendships." *American Sociological Review* 43 (April 1978): 237-250.

Edwards, Carolyn P., and Whiting, Beatrice B. "Women and Dependency." *Politics and Society* 4, no. 3 (1974).

Edwards, Richard C. "Personal Traits and 'Success' in Schooling and Work." *Educational and Psychological Measurement* 37 (Spring 1977): 125-138.

Ehrenreich, Barbara, and Stallard, Karen. "The Nouveau Poor." *Ms.*, August 1982.

Eisenstein, Zillah. *The Radical Future of Liberal Feminism*. New York: Longman, 1981.

———, ed. *Capitalist Patriarchy and the Case for Socialist Feminism*. New York: Monthly Review Press, 1979.

Ekstrand, Laurie E., and Eckert, William A. "The Impact of Candidates' Sex on Voter Choice." *Western Political Quarterly* 35 (March 1981).

Elshtain, Jean Bethke. *The Family in Political Thought*. Amherst: University of Massachusetts Press, 1982.

———. "The Feminist Movement and the Question of Equality." *Polity* 7 (Summer 1975).

———. "Kant, Politics, and Persons: The Implications of His Moral Philosophy." *Polity* 14 (Winter 1982).

———. "Moral Woman/Immoral Man: The Public/Private Distinction and Its Political Ramifications." *Politics and Society* 4 (1974).

———. *Public Man, Private Woman*. Princeton, N.J.: Princeton University Press, 1981.

English, Jane, ed. *Sex Equality*. Englewood Cliffs, N.J.: Prentice-Hall, 1977.

Eulau, Heinz. *The Behavioral Persuasion in Politics*. New York: Random House, 1967.

Eulau, Heinz; Whalke, John C.; Buchanan, William; and Ferguson, Leroy C. "The Role of the Representative: Some Empirical Observations in the Theory of Edmund Burke." *American Political Science Review* (September 1959).

Evans, Judith. "Women and Politics: A Re-Appraisal." *Political Studies* 28 (June 1980): 210-221.

Evans, Sara. *Personal Politics.* New York: Vintage Books, 1979.

Feagin, J. R. "Social Sources of Support for Violence and Nonviolence in the Negro Ghetto." *Social Problems* 15 (Spring 1968): 425-460.

Feagin, Joe R., and Feagin, Clairece Booker. *Discrimination American Style: Institutional Racism and Sexism.* Englewood Cliffs, N.J.: Prentice-Hall, 1978.

Featherman, David L., and Hauser, Robert M. "Sexual Inequalities and Socioeconomic Achievement in the U.S., 1962-1973." *American Sociological Review* 41 (June 1976): 462-483.

Ferber, Marianne A.; Loeb, Jane W.; and Lowry, Helen M. "The Economic Status of Women Faculty: A Reappraisal." *Journal of Human Resources* 13 (Summer 1978): 385-401.

Ferber, Marianne A., and Lowry, Helen M. "The Sex Difference in Earnings: A Reappraisal," *Industrial and Labor Relations Review* 29 (July 1976): 377-387.

Ferber, Marianne A., and McMahon, Walter W. "Women's Expected Earnings and Their Investment in Higher Education." *Journal of Human Resources* 14 (Summer 1979).

Finn, Ed. "Equal Rights: Fact or Fantasy? *Labour Gazette* (May 1978).

Firestone, Shulamith. *The Dialectic of Sex: The Case for Feminist Revolution.* New York: Bantam Books, 1970.

Fisher, Christine. "Women's Battles for Equal Rights." *Labour Gazette* (May 1978).

Flaming, Karl H.; Palen, J. John; Ringlien, Grant; and Taylor, Corneff. "Black Powerlessness in Policy-Making Positions." In *City Scenes*, edited by J. John Palen. Boston: Little, Brown & Co., 1977.

Flanagan, Robert J. "Actual versus Potential Impact of Government Antidiscrimination Programs." *Industrial and Labor Relations Review* 29 (July 1976).

Flatham, Richard E. "Equality and Generalization: A Formal Analysis." In *Nomos IX, Equality*, edited by J. Roland Pennock and John W. Chapman. New York: Atherton Press, 1967.

———. "Rights, Needs, and Liberalism: A Comment on Bay." *Political Theory* 8 (August 1980).

Fogelson, Robert M. "From Resentment to Confrontation: The Police, the Negroes, and the Outbreak of the Nineteen-Sixties Riots." *Political Science Quarterly* 83 (June 1968).

———. "Violence as Protest." In *Urban Riots, Violence, and Social Change*, edited by Robert Connery. New York: Vintage Books, 1967.

Fowler, Robert Booth, and Orenstein, Jeffery R. *Contemporary Issues in Political Theory.* New York: John Wiley & Sons, 1977.

Fowlkes, Diane L. "Ambitious Political Woman: Countersocialization and Political Party Context." Presented at the Annual Meeting of the Midwest Political Science Association. Cincinnati, Ohio, April 16-18, 1981.

Fowlkes, Diane; Perkins, Jerry; and Rhinehart, Sue Tolleson. "Gender Roles and Party Roles." *American Political Science Review* 73 (September 1979): 772-780.

Frank, Alan H.; Berman, John J.; and Mazur-Hart, Stanley F. "No-Fault Divorce and the Divorce Rate: The Nebraska Experience—An Interrupted Time Series Analysis and Commentary." *Nebraska Law Review* 58, no. 1 (1978): 1-99.

Frankena, William K. "The Concept of Social Justice." In *Social Justice*, ed. Richard B. Brandt, pp. 1-29. Englewood Cliffs, N.J.: Prentice-Hall, 1962.

Frankovic, Kathleen A. "Sex and Voting in the U.S. House of Representatives, 1961-1975." *American Politics Quarterly* 5 (July 1977): 315-330.

Freed, Doris Jonas, and Foster, Henry H., Jr. "Divorce in the Fifty States: An Overview." *Family Law Quarterly* 14 (Winter 1981): 229-283.

Freeman, Bonnie Cook. "Power, Patriarchy, and 'Political Primitives.' " In *Beyond Intellectual Sexism: A New Woman, New Reality*, edited by Joan I. Roberts, pp. 241-264. New York: David McKay Co., 1976.

Freeman, Jo. "The Origins of the Women's Liberation Movement." *American Journal of Society* 78 (January 1973): 792-811.

―――. *The Politics of Women's Liberation*. New York: David McKay Co., 1975.

―――, ed. *Women: A Feminist Perspective*. Palo Alto, Calif.: Mayfield, 1975.

Furlenwider, Claire Knoche. *Feminism in American Politics: A Study of Ideological Influence*. New York: Praeger, 1980.

Galowitz, Paula. "Poor Women and Housing." *Clearinghouse Review/National Clearinghouse for Legal Services* 14 (February 1981): 1060-1064.

Gans, Herbert. *More Equality*. New York: Vintage Books, 1973.

―――. "Some Problems of Equality." *Dissent* 20 (Fall 1973): 409-414.

Gehlen, Frieda L. "Women in Congress." *Transaction*, October 1969, pp. 36-40.

―――. "Women Members of Congress: A Distinctive Role." In *A Portrait of Marginality: The Political Behavior of the American Woman*, edited by Marianne Githens and Jewel L. Prestage, pp. 304-319. New York: David McKay Co., 1977.

Gelb, Joyce, and Palley, Marian Lief. "Women and Interest Group Politics: A Case Study of the Equal Credit Opportunity Act." *American Politics Quarterly* 5 (July 1977): 331-352.

―――. "Women and Interest Group Politics: A Comparative Analysis of Federal Decision-Making." *Journal of Politics* 41, no 2 (May 1979): 362-392.

Georgakas, Dan, and Surkin, Marvin. *Detroit, I Do Mind Dying*. New York: St. Martin's Press, 1975.

Gillespie, Dorie L. "Who Has the Power: The Marital Struggle." In *Women: A Feminist Perspective*, edited by Jo Freeman, pp. 64-67. Palo Alto, Calif.: Mayfield, 1975.

Ginzberg, Eli. "The Job Problem." *Scientific American*, November 1977, pp. 43-50.

Gitelson, Alan R., and Gitelson, Idy B. "Adolescents' Attitudes toward Male and Female Political Candidates." Presented at the Annual Meeting of the Southern Political Science Association. Atlanta, Ga., November 1976.

Githens, Marianne. "Spectators, Agitators, or Lawmakers: Women in State Legislatures." In *A Portrait of Marginality: The Political Behavior of the American Woman*, edited by Marianne Githens and Jewel L. Prestage, pp. 196-210. New York: David McKay Co., 1977.

Githens, Marianne, and Prestage, Jewel L., eds. *A Portrait of Marginality: The Political Behavior of the American Woman*. New York: David McKay Co., 1977.

Glazer, Nona, and Waehrer, Helen Youngelson, eds. *Woman in a Man-Made World*. 2d ed. Chicago: Rand McNally, 1977.

Goldstein, Morris, and Smith, Robert S. "The Estimated Impact of the Antidiscrimination Program Aimed at Federal Contractors." *Industrial and Labor Relations Review* 29 (July 1976): 523-543.

Goodin, Robert E. "Notes and Comments: Convention Quotas and Communal Representation." *British Journal of Political Science* 7 (1977): 255-272.

Goodwin, Barbara. "Utopia Defended against the Liberals." *Political Studies* 28 (September 1980): 384-400.

Gordon, Linda, and Erlien, Marla. "The Politics of Puritanism." *The Nation*, November 28, 1981.

Gornick, Vivian, and Moran, Barbara K., eds. *Women in a Sexist Society*. New York: New American Library, 1971.

Gought, Kathleen. "The Origin of the Family." In *Women: A Feminist Perspective*, edited by Jo Freeman, pp. 43-63. Palo Alto, Calif.: Mayfield, 1975.

Graeme, Duncan, and Lukes, Steven. "Democracy Restated." In *Frontiers of Democratic Theory*, edited by Henry S. Kariel, pp. 188-213. New York: Random House, 1970.

Gray, John N. "On Negative and Positive Liberty." *Political Studies* 28 (December 1980): 507-526.

Green, Philip, and Dahl, Robert A. "What Is Political Equality?" *Dissent* 25 (Summer 1979): 351-368.

Greenman, Antonia M. "Women's Rights and State Legislatures." Washington, D.C.: American Family Institute, 1980.

Gutmann, Amy. "Public Schooling and Private Values: Should a Liberal State Remain Neutral in Education?" Presented at the Annual Meeting of the American Political Science Association. Washington, D.C., August 31-September 3, 1979.

Hacker, Sally. "Sex Stratification, Technology, and Organizational Change: A Longitudinal Case Study of AT&T." *Social Problems* 26, no. 5 (June 1979): 539-553.

Hanson, Susan B.; Frantz, Linda M.; and Netemeyer-Mays, Margaret. "Women's Political Participation and Policy Preferences." *Social Science Quarterly* 56, no. 4 (March 1976).

Harvard Law Review. "Sex Discrimination and Equal Protection: Do We Need a Constitutional Amendment?" Vol. 84 (1971).

Hauser, Robert M. "Comment on Beck et al., ASR, October 1978, 'Stratification in a Dual Economy.'" *American Sociological Review* 45 (August 1980): 702-711.

Heckman, James J., and Wolpin, Kenneth I. "Does the Contract Compliance Program Work? An Analysis of Chicago Data."*Industrial and Labor Relations Review* 29 (July 1976): 544-564.

Hedges, Janice Neipert, and Mellor, Earl F. "Weekly and Hourly Earnings of U.S. Workers, 1967-78." *Monthly Labor Review* 102 (August 1979).

Hedlund, Ronald D.; Freeman, Patricia K.; Hamm, Keith E.; and Stein, Robert M. "The Electability of Women Candidates: The Effects of Sex Role Stereotypes." *Journal of Politics* 41 (May 1979): 513-524.

Heilbrun, Carolyn. *Toward a Recognition of Androgyny*. New York: Alfred A. Knopf, 1973.

Hershey, Marjorie Randon. "The Politics of Androgyny? Sex Roles and Attitudes toward Women in Politics." *American Politics Quarterly* 5 (July 1977): 261-287.

Hill, Robert, and Fogelson, Robert. "Who Riots? A Study of Participation in the 1967 Riots." *Supplemental Studies for the National Advisory Commission on Civil Disorders*. July 1968.

Howe, Louise Knapp. *Pink Collar Workers*. New York: Avon Books, 1977.

Huber, Joan, ed. *Changing Woman in a Changing Society*. Chicago: University of Chicago Press, 1973.

Huckle, Patricia. "The Womb Factor: Pregnancy Policies and Employment of Women." *Western Political Quarterly* 33 (June 1980).

Huitt, Ralph K. "The Outsider in the Senate: An Alternative Role." *American Political Science Review* 55, no. 3 (September 1961).

Iglitzen, Lynne B. "Political Education and Sexual Liberation." *Politics and Society* 2 (Winter 1972).

Jaggar, Alison. "On Sexual Equality." In *Sex Equality*, edited by Jane English, pp. 93-109. Englewood Cliffs, N.J.: Prentice-Hall, 1977.

Jaquette, Jane, ed. *Women in Politics*. New York: John Wiley & Sons, 1974.
Jennings, M. Kent, and Farah, Barbara G. "Ideology, Gender, and Political Action: A Cross-National Survey." *British Journal of Political Science* 10 (April 1980): 219-240.
Jennings, M. Kent, and Thomas, Norman. "Men and Women in Party Elites: Social Roles and Political Resources." *Midwest Journal of Political Science* 12 (November 1968).
Johnson, Beverly L. "Women Who Head Families, 1970-77: Their Numbers Rose, Income Lagged." *Monthly Labor Review* 101 (February 1978): 32-37.
Johnson, George E., and Welch, Finis. "The Labor Market Implications of an Economywide Affirmative Action Program." *Industrial and Labor Relations Review* 29 (July 1976): 508-522.
Johnson, Paula. "Women and Power: Towards a Theory of Effectiveness." *Journal of Social Issues* 32, no. 3 (1976).
Joreen. "The 51 Percent Minority Group: A Statistical Essay." In *Sisterhood Is Powerful*, edited by Robin Morgan, pp. 455-468. New York: Vintage Books, 1970.
Joseph, Lawrence B., "Some Ways of Thinking about Equality of Opportunity." *Western Political Quarterly* 33 (September 1980): 393-400.
Kanowitz, Leo. *Women and the Law: The Unfinished Revolution*. Albuquerque: University of New Mexico Press, 1969.
Kariel, Henry S. *Frontiers of Democratic Theory*. New York: Random House, 1970.
Katzenmeyer, W. G., and Stenner, A. Jackson. "Estimation of the Invariance of Factor Structures across Sex and Race with Implications for Hypothesis Testing." *Educational and Psychological Measurement* 37 (Spring 1977):111-119.
Kincade, Diane D. "Over His Dead Body: A Positive Perspective on Widows in the United States Congress." *Western Political Quarterly* 31 (1978): 96-104.
King, Elizabeth G. "Women in Iowa Legislative Politics." In *A Portrait of Marginality: The Political Behavior of the American Woman*, edited by Marianne Githens and Jewel L. Prestage, pp. 284-303. New York: David McKay Co., 1977.
Kirkpatrick, Jeane. "Representatives in the American National Conventions: The Case of 1972." *British Journal of Political Science* 5 (1975): 265-322.
Kreps, Juanita. *Sex in the Market Place: American Women at Work*. Baltimore: Johns Hopkins University Press, 1971.
Kreps, Juanita, and Clark, Robert. *Sex, Age, and Work: The Changing Composition of the Labor Force*. Baltimore: Johns Hopkins University Press, 1975.

Lang, Dorothy T. "Poor Women and Health Care." *Clearinghouse Review/ National Clearinghouse for Legal Services* 14 (February 1981): 1056-1060.
Lang, Kurt, and Lang, Gladys Engel. "Racial Disturbances as Collective Protest." *American Behavioral Scientist* 11 (March-April 1968).
Lansing, Marjorie, and Baxter, Sandra. *Women and Politics: The Invisible Majority*. Ann Arbor: University of Michigan Press, 1981.
Lee, Marcia Manning. "Why Few Women Hold Public Office: Democracy and Sexual Roles." *Political Science Quarterly* 91 (Summer 1976): 297-314.
Lever, Janet. "Sex Differences in the Complexity of Children's Play and Games." *American Sociological Review* 43 (August 1978): 471-482.
Lloyd, Cynthia; Andrews, Emily; and Gilroy, Curtis L. *Women in the Labor Market*. New York: Columbia University Press, 1979.
Lombardi, Vincent L. *Crisis in Marriage: Efforts toward Spiritual Transformation*. Washington, D.C.: University Press of America, 1981.
Lord, Robert G.; Phillips, James S.; and Rush, Michael C. "Effects of Sex and Personality on Perceptions of Emergent Leadership, Influence, and Social Power." *Journal of Applied Psychology* 65 (April 1980): 176-182.
Lynn, Naomi. "Women in American Politics: An Overview." In *Women: A Feminist Perspective*, edited by Jo Freeman, pp. 366-367. Palo Alto, Calif.: Mayfield, 1975.
McClendon, McKee J. "The Occupational Status Attainment Processes of Males and Females." *American Sociological Review* 41 (February 1976): 52-64.
McDonagh, Eileen L. "To Work or Not to Work: The Differential Impact of Achieved and Derived Status upon the Political Participation of Women, 1956-1976." *American Journal of Political Science* 26 (May 1982): 280-297.
McDonald, Beverly Leopold, and Diehl, Rita. "Women and Welfare." *Clearinghouse Review/National Clearinghouse for Legal Services* 14 (February, 1981): 1036-1041.
McLaughlin, Steven D. "Occupational Sex Identification and the Assessment of Male and Female Earnings Inequality." *American Sociological Review* 43 (December 1978): 909-921.
MacManus, Susan A. "A City's First Female Officeholder: 'Coattails' for Future Female Officeseekers?" *Western Political Quarterly* 34 (March 1981): 88-99.
Macpherson, C. B. "Class, Classlessness, and the Critique of Rawls: A Reply to Nielsen." *Political Theory* 6 (May 1978): 209-211.
―――. *Democratic Theory: Essays in Retrieval*. London: Oxford University Press, 1973.

———. *The Life and Times of Liberal Democracy*. London: Oxford University Press, 1977.
———. *The Real World of Democracy*. London: Oxford University Press, 1971.
Maguire, Daniel. *A New American Justice*. Garden City, N.Y.: Doubleday and Co. 1980.
Mansbridge, Jane J. "Time, Emotion, and Inequality: Three Problems of Participatory Groups." *Journal of Applied Behavioral Science* 9 (1973): 351-368.
Marini, Margaret Mooney. "The Transition to Adulthood: Sex Differences in Educational Attainment and Age at Marriage." *American Sociological Review* 43 (August 1978): 483-507.
Mason, Karen Oppenheim; Czajka, John L.; and Arbor, Sara. "Change in U.S. Women's Sex-Role Attitudes, 1964-1974." *American Sociological Review* 41 (August 1976): 573-596.
Mayer, Helen Hacker. "Women as a Minority Group." In *Women: A Feminist Perspective*, edited by Jo Freeman, pp. 402-415. Palo Alto, Calif.: Mayfield, 1975.
Mayo, Henry B. *An Introduction to Democratic Theory*. New York: Oxford University Press, 1960.
Mednick, Martha T. Shuch; Tangri, Sandra Schwartz; and Hoffman, Lois Wladis, eds. *Women and Achievement: Social and Motivational Analysis*. New York: John Wiley & Sons, Halsted Press, 1975.
Merritt, Shayne. "Winners and Losers: Sex Differences in Municipal Elections." *American Journal of Political Science* 21, no. 4 (November 1977): 731-743.
Mezey, Susan Gluck. "Support for Women's Rights Policies: An Analysis of Local Politicians." *American Politics Quarterly* 6 (October 1978): 485-497.
Mill, John Stuart, and Taylor, Harriet. *Essays on Sex Equality*. Chicago: University of Chicago Press, 1970.
Miller, Lawrence W., and Noyes, Lillian F. "Winners and Losers: Women Candidates for Municipal Elections Revisited." Presented at the Annual Meeting of the Midwest Political Science Association. Chicago, Ill., April 24-26, 1980.
Miller, Warren E., and Stokes, Donald E. "Constituency Influence in Congress." *American Political Science Review* (March 1963): 45-56.
Mills, C. W. *The Sociological Imagination*. London: Oxford University Press, 1959.
Mincer, Jacob, and Polachek, Solomon. "Women's Earnings Re-examined." *Journal of Human Resources* 13 (Winter 1978): 118-134.
Mitchell, Juliet. *Psycho-Analysis and Feminism*. New York: Vintage Books, 1974.

———. *Women's Estate*. New York: Vintage Books, 1970.
Moore, Barrington. "Thoughts on Violence and Democracy." In *Urban Riots, Violence and Social Change*, edited by Robert Connery, pp. 3-15. New York: Vintage Books, 1967.
Morgan, Robin. *Going Too Far: The Personal Chronical of a Feminist*. New York: Vintage Books, 1978.
———. *Sisterhood Is Powerful*. New York: Vintage Books, 1970.
Nelson, Bruce A.; Opton, Edward M., Jr.; and Wilson, Thomas E. "Wage Discrimination and the 'Comparable Worth' Theory in Perspective." *Journal of Law Reform* 13 (Winter 1980): 231-301.
Newton, Lisa. "Reverse Discrimination as Unjustified." In *Sex Equality*, edited by Jane English, pp. 155-160. Englewood Cliffs, N.J.: Prentice-Hall, 1977.
Nichols, Mary P. "Women in Western Political Thought." Presented at the Annual Meeting of the Midwest Political Science Association. Milwaukee, Wis., April 29-May 1, 1982.
Nieburg, H. K. "Violence, Law, and Social Process." In *Riots and Rebellion: Civil Violence in the Urban Community*, edited by Lewis H. Masotti and Don R. Bowen, pp. 379-389. Beverly Hills, California: Sage, 1968.
Nielsen, Kai. "On the Very Possibility of a Classless Society: Rawls, Macpherson, and Revisionist Liberalism." *Political Theory* 6 (May 1978): 191-208.
Niemi, Albert W., Jr. "Discrimination against Women Reconsidered." *American Journal of Economics and Sociology* 38 (July 1979): 291-292.
Niemi, Richard G.; Hedges, Roman; and Jennings, M. Kent. "The Similarity of Husbands' and Wives' Political Views." *American Politics Quarterly* 5 (April 1977): 133-148.
Norgren, Jill. "In Search of a National Child Care Policy: Background and Prospects." *Western Political Quarterly* 34 (March 1981): 127-142.
O'Kelly, Charlotte. "The 'Impact' of Equal Employment Legislation on Women's Earnings: Limitations of Legislative Solutions to Discrimination in the Economy." *American Journal of Sociology* 38, no. 4 (October 1979): 419-429.
Okin, Susan Moller. *Women in Western Political Thought*. Princeton, N.J.: Princeton University Press, 1979.
O'Neill, Onora. "How Do We Know When Opportunities Are Equal?" in *Sex Equality*, edited by Jane English, pp. 143-154. Englewood Cliffs, N.J.: Prentice-Hall, 1977.
Oppenheimer, Valerie Kincade. "Demographic Influence on Female Employment and the Status of Women." In *Changing Woman in a Changing Society*, edited by Joan Huber, pp. 184-199. Chicago: University of Chicago Press, 1973.

Oppenheim, Felix E. "Egalitarian Rules of Distribution." *Ethics* 90 (January 1980): 164-179.
Orum, Anthony; Cohen, Roberta S.; Grasmuck, Sherri; and Orum, Amy W. "Sex, Socialization, and Politics." *American Sociological Review* 39 (April 1974): 197-208.
Pateman, Carole. "The Disorder of Women: Women, Love, and the Sense of Justice." *Ethics* 91 (October 1980): 20-34.
———. *Participation and Democratic Theory*. Cambridge: Cambridge University Press, 1970.
———. "Sublimation and Reification: Locke, Wolin, and the Liberal Democratic Conception of the Political." *Politics and Society* 6 (1975): 441-467.
———. "Women and Consent." *Political Theory* 8 (May 1980): 149-168.
———. "Women, Nature, and the Suffrage." *Ethics* 90 (July 1980): 564-575.
Pennock, J. Roland, and Chapman, John W., eds. *Nomos IX: Equality*. New York: Atherton Press, 1967.
Perkins, Jerry, and Fowlkes, Diane L. "Opinion Representation versus Social Representation; or, Why Women Can't Run as Women and Win." *American Political Science Review* 74, no. 1 (March 1980): 92-103.
Piercy, Marge. *Small Changes*. New York: Fawcett Crest Books, 1972.
———. *Woman on the Edge of Time*. New York: Fawcett Crest Books, 1976.
Pitkin, Hannah Fenichel. *The Concept of Representation*. Berkeley: University of California Press, 1967.
Powell, Lynda Watts. "Male and Female Differences in Elite Political Participation: An Examination of the Effects of Socioeconomics and Familial Variables." *Western Political Quarterly* 34 (March, 1981): 31-45.
Power, Sarah Goddard. "Women, the Economy, and the Future." University of Michigan School of Education, *University Innovator* 13 (September 1981).
Prewitt, Kenneth, and Stone, Alan. *The Ruling Elite*. New York: Harper & Row, 1973.
Quarantelli, E. D., and Dynes, Russell. "Looting in Civil Disorders: An Index of Social Change." *American Behavioral Scientist* 11 (March-April 1968): 7-10.
Ransford, H. Edward. "Isolation, Powerlessness, and Violence: A Study of Attitudes and Participation in the Watts Riot." *American Journal of Sociology* 73 (March 1968).
Rawls, John. *A Theory of Justice*. Cambridge: Harvard University Press, Belknap Press, 1971.
Reich, Michael. "Who Benefits from Racism? The Distribution among Whites of Gains and Losses from Racial Inequality." *Journal of Human Resources* 13 (Fall 1978): 524-544.

Remick, Helen. "IRC Colloquium on Job Evaluation and EEO: The Emerging Issues; Strategies for Creating Sound, Bias-Free Job Evaluation Plans." Presented at Industrial Relations Counselors, Inc., Symposium on Job Evaluation and EEO: The Emerging Issues. Atlanta, Ga., September 14 and 15, 1978.

Reskin, Barbara F. "Sex Differences in Status Attainment in Science: The Case of the Postdoctoral Fellowship." *American Sociological Review* 41 (August 1976): 597-612.

Rosenfeld, Rachel A. "Women's Intergenerational Occupational Mobility." *American Sociological Review* 43 (February 1978): 36-46.

Rossi, Alice. "Sex Equality: The Beginning of Ideology." In *Masculine/Feminine: Readings in Sexual Mythology and the Liberation of Women*, edited by Betty Roszak and Theodore Roszak, pp. 173-183. New York: Harper Colophon Books, 1969.

Roszak, Betty. "The Human Continuum." In *Masculine/Feminine: Readings in Sexual Mythology and the Liberation of Women*, edited by Betty Roszak and Theodore Roszak, pp. 297-306. New York: Harper Colophon Books, 1969.

Roszak, Betty, and Roszak, Theodore, eds. *Masculine/Feminine: Readings in Sexual Mythology and the Liberation of Women*. New York: Harper Colophon Books, 1969.

Rothman, Sheila. *Women's Proper Place*. New York: Basic Books, 1978.

Rowbotham, Sheila. *Women, Resistance, and Revolution*. New York: Vintage Books, 1974.

Rule, Wilma. "Why Women Don't Run: The Critical Contextual Factors in Women's Legislative Recruitment." *Western Political Quarterly* 34 (March 1981): 60-77.

Rumberger, Russell W., and Carney, Martin. "Segmentation in the U.S. Labour Market: Its Effects on the Mobility and Earnings of Whites and Blacks." *Cambridge Journal of Economics* 4 (June 1980): 117-132.

Ryan, William. *Equality*. New York: Vintage Books, 1982.

Sandell, Steven H., and Shapiro, David. "An Exchange: The Theory of Human Capital and the Earnings of Women, a Reexamination of the Evidence." *Journal of Human Resources* 13 (Winter 1978):103-117.

Sapiro, Virginia. "News from the Front: Intersex and Intergenerational Conflict over the Status of Women." *Western Political Quarterly* 33 (June 1980): 260-277.

―――. "Private Costs of Public Commitments or Public Costs of Private Commitments: Family Roles vs. Political Ambitions." *American Journal of Political Science* 26 (May 1982): 265-279.

―――. "Sex and Games: An Oppression and Rationality." *British Journal of Political Science* 9 (October 1979): 385-407.

———. "When Are Interests Interesting?" *American Political Science Review* 75, no. 3 (September 1981): 701-712.

Saxonhouse, Arlene W. "Men, Women, War, and Politics: Family and Polis in Aristophanes and Euripedes." *Political Theory* 8 (February 1980): 65-81.

Schaar, John H. "Equality of Opportunity, and Beyond." In *Nomos IX: Equality*, edited by J. Roland Pennock and John W. Chapman, pp. 228-249. New York: Atherton Press, 1967.

Schmitt, Neal, and Lappin, Martha. "Race and Sex as Determinants of the Mean and Variance of Performance Ratings." *Journal of Applied Psychology* 65 (August 1980): 428-435.

Schneier, Craig Eric, and Bartel, Kathryn M. "Short Notes: Sex Effects in Emergent Leadership." *Journal of Applied Psychology* 65 (June 1980): 341-345.

Schramm, Sarah Slavin. *Plow Women Rather than Reapers: An Intellectual History of Feminism in the United States*. Metuchen, N.J.: Scarecrow Press, 1979.

———. "Women and Representation: Self-Government and Role Change." *Western Political Quarterly* 34 (March 1981): 46-59.

Schulman, Jeanne. "Poor Women and Family Law." *Clearinghouse Review/ National Clearinghouse for Legal Services* 14 (February 1981): 1069-1074.

Schwartz, Nancy L. "Distinction between Public and Private Life: Marx on the zoon politiken." *Political Theory* 7 (May 1979): 245-266.

Seal, Karen. "A Decade of No-Fault Divorce: What It Has Meant Financially for Women in California." *Family Advocate* 1 (Spring 1979): 10-15.

Segers, Mary C. "Equality in Contemporary Political Thought: An Examination and an Assessment." *Administration and Society* 10 (February 1979): 409-436.

———. "Equality, Public Policy, and Relevant Sex Differences." *Polity* 2 (1979): 319-339.

Seidenberg, Faith A. "The Submissive Majority: Modern Trends in the Law concerning Women's Rights." *Cornell Law Review* 55 (1969-70).

Sepler, Harvey J. "Measuring the Effects of No-Fault Divorce Laws across Fifty States: Quantifying a Zeitgeist." *Family Law Quarterly* 15 (Spring 1981): 65-93.

Sewell, William H. "Social Mobility and Social Participation." *Annals of the American Academy of Political and Social Sciences* (January 1978): 230-235.

Shalala, Donna. "Women in Power: An Agenda for the Eighties." *Ms.*, May 1982, pp. 96-101.

Shariff, Zahid. "Intra-Family Equality and Income Distribution: Emerging Conflicts in Public Policy." *American Journal of Economics and Sociology* 38 (January 1979): 49-59.

Smith, Lee. "The EEOC's Bold Foray into Job Evaluation." *Fortune*, September 11, 1978, pp. 58-60.

Smith, Ralph. *The Subtle Revolution*. Washington, D.C.: Urban Institute, 1979.

Smith, Robert C. "Black Power and the Transformation from Protest to Politics." *Political Science Quarterly* 96 (Fall 1981): 431-443.

Snow, Charlene. "Women in Prison." *Clearinghouse Review/National Clearinghouse for Legal Services* 14 (February 1981): 1065-1068.

Sommers, Tish, and Shields, Laurie. "Displaced Homemakers' 'Forced Retirement' Leaves Many Penniless." *Civil Rights Digest* 10 (Winter 1978): 33-39.

Sontag, Susan. "On the Meaning of Margaret Thatcher." *Ms.*, July 1979, p. 68.

Soule, John W., and McGrath, Wilma E. "A Comparative Study of Male and Female Political Attitudes at Citizen and Elite Levels." In *A Portrait of Marginality: The Political Behavior of the American Woman*, edited by Marianne Githens and Jewel L. Prestage, pp. 178-195. New York: David McKay Co., 1977.

Stanley, John. "Equality of Opportunity as Philosophy and Ideology." *Political Theory* 5 (February 1977): 15-30.

Staudt, Kathleen A. "Class and Sex in the Politics of Women Farmers." *Journal of Politics* 41 (May 1979): 492-512.

Steinem, Gloria. "Post-ERA Politics: Losing a Battle but Winning the War?" *Ms.*, January 1983, pp. 65-66.

Stellman, Jeanne M. "The Hidden Health Toll: A Cost of Work to the American Woman." *Civil Rights Digest* 10 (Fall 1977): 32-41.

Stencel, Sandra. "The Changing American Family: The Women's Movement: Achievements and Effects." Editorial Research Reports, *Congressional Quarterly* (June 1977): 1-20.

———. "Single-Parent Families." Editorial Research Reports, *Congressional Quarterly* (June 1977): 63-82.

———. "Women in the Work Force." Editorial Research Reports *Congressional Quarterly* (June 1977): 21-42.

Stevenson, Mary H. "Women's Wages and Job Segregation." *Politics and Society* 4 (Fall 1973): 83-96.

Strum, Philippa. "Pink Collar Blues: For Women Who Work, It Still Doesn't Add Up." *Perspectives: The Civil Rights Quarterly* 12 (Summer 1980): 33-37.

Szymanski, Albert. "Racial Discrimination and White Gain." *American Sociological Review* 41 (June 1976): 403-414.

———. "Racism and Sexism as Functional Substitutes in the Labor Market." *Sociological Quarterly* 17 (Winter 1976): 65-73.

Tanner, Leslie B., ed. *Voices from Women's Liberation*. New York: New American Library, 1970.
Tedin, Kent; Brady, David W.; Buxton, Mary E.; German, Barbara M.; and Thompson, Judy L. "Social Background and Political Differences between Pro- and Anti-ERA Activists." *American Political Quarterly* 5 (July 1977): 395-408.
Thompson, Mary Lou, ed. *Voices of the New Feminism*. Boston: Beacon Press, 1970.
Thurow, Lester. *Generating Inequality*. New York: Basic Books, 1975.
Time Magazine. "The American Underclass: Destitute and Desperate in the Land of Plenty," August 29, 1977.
Tolchin, Susan and Martin. *Clout: Womanpower and Politics*. New York: Capricorn Books, 1973.
Trebilcot, Joyce. "Sex Roles: The Argument from Nature." *Ethics* 85 (April 1975): 245-255.
Treiman, Donald J., and Hartmann, Heidi I., eds. *Women, Work, and Wages*. Washington, D.C.: National Academy Press, 1981.
U.S. Commission on Civil Rights. *Toward Equal Educational Opportunity: Affirmative Admissions Programs at Law and Medical School*. Clearinghouse Publication 55 (June 1978).
———. *Unemployment and Underemployment among Blacks, Hispanics, and Women*. Clearinghouse Publication 74 (November 1982).
U.S. Department of Labor, Bureau of Labor Statistics. *Perspectives on Working Women: A Databook, Bulletin 2080*. Washington, D.C. (October, 1980).
U.S. Department of Labor, Women's Bureau. "Economic Responsibilities of Working Women." (September, 1979).
Van Dyke, Vernon. "Collective Entities and Moral Rights: Problems in Liberal-Democratic Thought." *Journal of Politics* 44 (February 1982): 21-40.
Van Hightower, Nikki R. "The Recruitment of Women for Public Office." *American Politics Quarterly* 5 (July 1977): 301-314.
Vlastos, Gregory. "Justice and Equality." In *Social Justice*, edited by Richard Brandt, pp. 31-72. Englewood Cliffs, N.J.: Prentice-Hall, 1962.
Waldman, Elizabeth, and McEddy, Beverly J. "Where Women Work: An Analysis by Industry and Occupation." *Monthly Labor Review* 97 (May 1974): 1-15.
Walker, Jack B. "Normative Consequences of Democratic Theory." In *Frontiers of Democratic Theory*, edited by Henry S. Kariel, pp. 227-247. New York: Random House, 1970.
Walker, Michael. "In Defense of Equality." *Dissent* 20 (Fall, 1973): 399-408.
Weiss, Shevach, and Yishai, Yael. "Women's Representation in Israeli Political Elites." *Jewish Social Studies* 62 (Spring 1980): 165-176.
Weitzman, Lenore. "Sex Role Socialization." In *Women: A Feminist Per-

spective, edited by Jo Freeman, pp. 105-144. Palo Alto, Calif.: Mayfield, 1975.

Weitzman, Lenore J., and Dixon, Ruth B. "The Alimony Myth: Does No-Fault Divorce Make a Difference?" *Family Law Quarterly* 14 (Fall, 1980): 141-185.

Welch, Susan. "Women as Political Animals? A Test of Some Explanations for Male-Female Political Participation Differences." *American Journal of Political Science* 21, no. 4 (November 1977): 711-730.

Welch, Susan, and Karnig, Albert K. "Correlates of Female Office Holding in City Politics." *Journal of Politics* 41 (May 1979): 478-491.

Welch, Susan, and Secret, Philip. "Sex, Race, and Political Participation." *Western Political Quarterly* 34 (March 1981): 5-16.

Werner, Emmy E. "Women in Congress, 1917-1964." *Western Political Quarterly* 19 (March 1966): 16-30.

———. "Women in the State Legislatures." *Western Political Quarterly* 21 (March 1968): 40-50.

Whalke, John C., and Eulau, Heinz. *The Legislative System*. New York: John Wiley & Sons, 1962.

Wheeler, Michael. *No-Fault Divorce*. Boston: Beacon Press, 1974.

White, Linda J. "Working Wives, 1940-1960." *American Sociological Review* 41 (February 1976): 65-79.

Williams, Bernard. "The Idea of Equality." In *Philosophy, Politics, and Society*, edited by Peter Laslett and W. G. Runciman, pp. 110-131. London: Oxford University Press, 1962.

Willis, Ellen. "Betty Friedan's 'Second Stage': A Step Backward." *Nation* 233 (November 14, 1981): 494-497.

Wilson, Anne; Bolt, Merry; and Larson, Wendy. "Women's Biology—Mankind's Destiny? The Population Explosion and Women's Changing Roles." In *Women: A Feminist Perspective*, edited by Jo Freeman, pp. 3-15. Palo Alto, Calif.: Mayfield, 1975.

Woods, Laurie. "The Challenge Facing Legal Services in the Eighties." December 15, 1981.

Young, Michael. "Is Equality a Dream?" *Dissent* 20 (Fall 1973): 415-422.

Zashin, Elliot M., "Affirmative Action and Federal Personnel Systems." *Public Policy* 28, no. 3 (Summer 1980): 351-380.

Index

Abortion, 14, 104
Abzug, Bella, 99
Academic qualifications, 81-82, 88n.40
Achievement, vicarious, 37-38
Affirmative action, 80-84
Affluent women, 15
Aged poor people, 54
American Telephone and Telegraph, 83-84
Amundsen, Kirsten, 30, 31, 72, 73, 96; on citizenship for disadvantaged groups, 98; institutional sexism concept, 58
Antifeminist women, in public office, 97
Antiwar movement, 102-3

Bank tellers, 54-55
Battered wives, 14
Berlin, Isaiah, 67
Birth control, 8, 50-51
Blacks: political activities of, 6; and socioeconomic change, 60; in urban politics, 107. *See also* Racism, institutional
Bryce, James, 93
Busing question, 79-80

Campaign funds, for women, 27-28
Candidates, women as, 27-28, 40, 95, 116n.22. *See also* Public office, women in
Carmichael, Stokely, 58
Childbearing, 50
Child-rearing responsibilities, 34-35, 40, 50-51
Children, and women's careers, 34-35
Child support, 52
Citizenship, and oppression, 29
Class identity of women, 57-58
Class system, sex-based, 8-9
Collective action by women, 14-15
Committee assignments, congressional, 26
Community life, participation in, 77
Competition among women, 14-15
Conflict, socialization of, 12
Congress, women in, 26, 40n.1, 94-95, 100, 106
Consciousness raising, 11
Croce, Jim, 57

Dahl, Robert, 112-13
Democracy, 110-11, 119-20n.78; and equality, 3, 15-16, 79
Democratic convention delegates, 104
Democratic theory, feminism and, 28, 107, 110-15

Dependency, in marriage, 47-48
Divorce, 51-52; no-fault, 84-85
Divorced women, 48

Economic changes, 14, 52-56
Economic conditions, and women's situations, 61
Economic dependency, in marriage, 48
Economic independence for women, 53
Economic inequalities, 6, 35-39
Edelman, Murray, 12, 107, 108
Educated women, jobs for, 56
Education: equality of, 73-74, 79-80; and income potential, 55; inequalities of, 6; and job discrimination, 39
Egalitarianism, negative, 66
Empirical observations, 17-18
Engels, Friedrich, 8
Equality, 65; as claim against inequality, 66, 86n.8; complete, 16, 22n.55; conditions of, 113-14; demands for, 3; as equal consideration of interest, 65-71; as impartiality, 67-68; of opportunity, 71-76; political, 15-16, 25; of results, 76-85, 112-13; sexual, 3-4; of treatment, 66-67. *See also* Inequalities
Equal pay, 68-69
Equal Pay Act, 36
Equal Rights Amendment, 96, 103, 105
Exploitation, 29

Family: functional differences in, 69-70; roles in, 84, 86n.8; social change and, 47-52; woman's role in, 18, 32-35
Female nature, 30-32
Feminine people, 22n.45

Feminine traits, 31; and job qualifications, 83
Feminine values, 72, 73
Feminism, 7; and childbearing, 50-51; and democratic theory, 28, 111-15; and family roles, 47-48, 50; goals of, 8; and inequalities, 78-79, 85; and oppression, 29; and political equality, 25, 77-78; and political participation by women, 9-15; and public office, 98-99; and qualifications for jobs, 82; and representation, 109-10; views of, 12; and voting rights, 92
Fertility control, 8, 50-51
Firestone, Shulamith, 8, 12, 29, 30, 72
Franchise, and women's equality, 29-30
Freeman, Jo, 8, 11-12, 95, 103, 105

Gender, and political attitudes, 4-5
Gender-related political participation, 12-13
Girls, training of, 31, 72
Goals, 4, 19n.5, 115
Good life: concern for, 13; equal rights to, 76-78
Green, Edith, 100
Griffiths, Martha, 100

Hamilton, Charles, 58
Hanse, Julia Butler, 100
Hershey, Marjorie Randon, 95
Holtzman, Liz, 100
Housewives, 49
Huitt, Ralph, 99-100

Impartiality, equality as, 67-68
Incomes, comparative, 39, 52, 53, 55. *See also* Wages of women
Independence of women, 48-49

Indirect achievement, 37-38
Inequalities: choice between, 70-71; equality as claim against, 66; increase in, 60-61; interrelation of, 18; political, 8-9, 25; political, economic dimension of, 35-39; political, solutions to, 9-15; and power, 75; social, 56
Institutional discrimination, 58-60
Institutions: political, influences on, 94-95; social, 56-60
Intellectual sophistication, and inequality, 16-17
Interest groups, 101, 102-7
Interests, equal consideration of, 65-71

Job discrimination, 36, 39-40, 55-56. *See also* Occupational segregation
Job market, sex-segregated, 36-37
Jobs: economic discrimination in, 35-39; high-paying, women in, 35; inequality of, 13, 15; for women, 32, 33-34. *See also* Women's work

Kassenbaum, Nancy Landon, 26
Kennedy, John F., 97

Labor force, women in, 52-53, 54
Legislators, women as, 94. *See also* Congress, women in
Librarians, sex discrimination among, 38-39
Lobbying, 105-6
Love, romantic, 72

Macpherson, C. B., 28
Majority rule, problems of, 114
Marriage, women's dependency in, 48
Masculine traits, 22n.45, 31

Meissner, Doris, 101
Men: oppression of women by, 8-9; power of, 8; social status of, 58; work of, 50
Mencken, H. L., 13
Merit, considerations of, 74
Mill, John Stuart, 3
Minorities, rights of, 114
Mitchell, Juliet, 7, 11, 78; on child-rearing, 51; on family roles, 49, 69; on male domination, 8-9; on women's relationships, 14-15
Mothers: of small children, 15; working, 51

Ninety-fourth Congress, 26
No-fault divorce, 84-85
Nominations, political, 101-2
Normative analysis, 17

Occupational segregation, 6, 36-39, 54-56, 58-60, 69
Officeholders, 94-95; female (*see* Public office, women in)
Office holding, 93-100
Older women, 48
Opportunity, equality of, 71-76
Oppressed persons, as citizens, 29
Oppression, 6, 29; and equality, 28; and female nature, 31-32; politicization of, 10; repression of words, 11; sexual, 8-9, 14

Participation, political, by women, 7-15; manipulation of, 107-8; voting, 91-93
Participatory democracy, 111
Parties. *See* Political party organizations
Pay, equality of, 9. *See also* Wages of women
Personality traits, sex-related, 31-32, 72

Personal relationships, 72
Philosophy, political, 19n.5
Pitkin, Hannah, 109, 110
Pluralism, 111
Policies: development by interest groups, 104; evaluation of, 79, 112
Political convention delegates, women as, 104
Political equality, 3-4, 15-16, 91; and democratic theory, 112; voting, 91-93
Political inequalities, 8-9, 25; economic dimension of, 35-39; in public office, 25-28; solutions to, 9-15
Political party organizations, 117n.35; women in, 27, 32, 101-2
Political philosophy, 19n.5
Political process, 108, 111-12, 115
Political views, sex differences in, 5
Politicization: of issues, 10, 12; of women, 103
Politics, as masculine activity, 12-13
Potential voting power, 92
Poverty: of blacks, 60; of women, 39, 48, 52, 53-54
Power, political, 98, 110; divisions of, 9-10; and inequality, 13; potential, of women voters, 92
Preferential treatment, 80-84
Pregnant women, discrimination against, 33
Private concerns, politicization of, 13-14, 104
Procedural democracy, 112-13
Professional women, 37
Public issues, 13-14
Public life, equality for women in, 82
Public office, women in, 25-26, 32, 34, 40, 93-100, 107, 109; number needed, 110

Qualifications, 80-83

Race, and political attitudes, 5
Race discrimination, and equal consideration of interest, 70
Racism, institutional, 58-60
Rawls, John, 35-36, 74
Representation, political, 101; of blacks, 6; of women, 4, 5, 8-10, 93-97, 99, 109-10
Representative government, 93-94
Reproductive rights, 14. *See also* Birth control
Responsibilities, gender-related, 5
Results, equality of, 4, 76-85
Reverse discrimination, 67, 81
Role models, 97-98
Roles: in family, 32-35, 47-52, 70; gender-related, 5, 22n.45; political, attitudes to, 95; in public office, 25, 99-100; sexual, and public office, 34-35; at work, 37
Romantic love, 72

Salaries, comparative, 39, 53. *See also* Wages of women
Sameness of treatment, 13, 66-67
Sapiro, Virginia, 81
Schaar, John, 71, 73
Schroeder, Pat, 100
Seal, Karen, 85
Self-confidence, and job qualification, 80-81
Self-image of women, 11, 32, 48
Sexism, institutional, 58-60
Sexual equality, 3-4; and political equality, 18
Single-parent families, 51-52
Social change, 47-64
Social inequality, 28-35
Social institutions, and discrimination, 56-60
Socialization of children, 31, 51, 72

Social position, assessment of, 29
Social representation, 96-97
Social Security benefits, for women, 48
Social stratification, 56-60
Standards, 4, 19n.5
Status quo, 4, 115
Sterilization, forced, 14
Sullivan, Lenor K., 100
Supervisory positions, women in, 38

Teachers, sex discrimination among, 38-39
Temperamental differences, sex-related, 30
Thatcher, Margaret, 97

Unions, women and, 15

Values, 4, 19n.5; hierarchy of, 73
Volunteers, political, 27
Voting, 91-93, 108; women and, 29-30

Wages of women, 35, 38, 39, 53-54, 84; comparative, 39, 53, 63n.32
Wives, 21n.18, 88n.41
Women: class identity of, 57-58; economic discrimination, 35-39; educated, jobs for, 56; family roles, 32-35, 47-52, 70; interests of, 12-13; in labor force, 52-53; political activity of, 101, 118n.43; political inequality of, 8-9; political inequality of, solutions to, 9-15; political participation of, 10, 107-8; politicization of, 103; in public office, 25-26, 32, 34, 40, 93-100, 107, 109, 110; self-confidence of, 40; self-image of, 11, 32, 48; views of other women, 32; voting of, 91-93; working mothers, 51; young mothers, 15
Women's issues, 4-7
Women's movement, 7, 11-12, 102-7. *See also* Feminism
Women's Political Caucus, 103
Women's work, 31-32, 36-38, 49, 55-56
Workers, women, 15
Work force, groups absent from, 15
Working mothers, 51

About the Author

Mary Lou Kendrigan is Assistant Professor in the Department of Social Science at Michigan State University. She is currently working on *Women, Political Equality, and the Military* for Greenwood Press and on studies of the impact on women of Compensation for Victims of Crime Programs, Rousseau's contribution to feminism, and Belle LaFollette and contemporary feminists.